ORDINARY STORIES

EXTRAORDINARY NARY GOD

Ordinary Stories, Extraordinary God

Copyright © 2024 Renee Gilmour

All rights reserved. No part of this book may be reproduced or used in any manner without the prior written permission of Renee Gilmour.

"Scripture quotations are from the ESV® Bible (The Holy Bible, English Standard Version®), © 2001 by Crossway, a publishing ministry of Good News Publishers. Used by permission. All rights reserved. The ESV text may not be quoted in any publication made available to the public by a Creative Commons license. The ESV may not be translated in whole or in part into any other language."

ISBN 978-0-646-89987-9

Printed in Australia
First edition 2024

Cover Art and Design:
Claire Hass

Editor:
Ruth Pereira

Readers and Encouragers:
Nath, Chloe, Sophie, Anna, Emma, Win, Roslyn, Michelle, Angela and Madeleine

Fact Checkers and Encouragers:
Kissa, Mandy and my Mum

For Phoebe, Holly, Elisha and Eve
May these ordinary stories of life
point you to great truths about our
extraordinary God.

In honour of my
Grandad Gibbons.

Contents

Introduction: Ordinary Stories of Europe 1
A Father's Applause 5
Hide and Seek 9
Bugle Bogas 13
Bag Carrier 17
Sickness Benefits 21
Glow Worm 25
Night Sky 29
Top Dog 33
Lady Shave 37
Mail Box 41
Hungry Jacks Origins 45
The Proposal 49
New Lenses 53
Fell Off in My Hand 57
Hearty Hospitality 61
Blinding Experiences 65

Familiar Paths 69
Sweet Surprises 73
Abey and Fluffy... 79
Tonsils Twice... 83
Zoe Monster Moments 87
Audacious Requests 91
Prickly Pear 95
The Wedgie... 99
Stuck Finger.. 103
King Mao 107
Undistracted Life 113
Carnival Parade 117
Special Heirlooms.. 121
Pet Show 125
Mighty America... 129
Aussie Accents 133
Boiling Kettle 137
Magical Worlds.. 141
References... 146
Scripture Index 147

Ordinary Stories of Europe

When I was 21, my sister and I travelled to England and parts of Europe. She had just completed her university degree and I had six months left of mine. My sister wanted to travel one last time before she got married later that year, and since our brother lived in London at the time, she decided it would be relatively inexpensive as we'd have free accommodation. I initially told her that I couldn't go with her because I was trying to save the little money that I had. Ignoring my reluctance, my sister went to a travel agent, booked two return tickets to London and told me how much I owed her for my ticket. She knew that I would never have booked it myself and assured me that I wouldn't regret it. Thankfully, she knew me well and I have never regretted those three weeks of memories and stories.

Knowing that I was tight with my money and that I would

have booked the cheapest possible flight, my sister booked us on a flight that had layovers in Sydney, Singapore and Paris. We were in transit for about 55 hours in total and during the second layover, I remember her asking me if I would have paid the extra five hundred dollars for a more direct route. By that stage in the journey, it was easy to reply with a resounding "Yes!" My brother and his girlfriend picked us up from Heathrow Airport and were excited to act as our travel guides in London. Because my brother had moved out of home when I was only 14 years old and had lived away or abroad after that, we didn't know each other well as adults. This holiday in Europe was the time that formed some of my greatest memories with him.

Over the next three weeks, we saw lots of popular tourist attractions in London and spent time together at a ski resort in Andorra (between France and Spain). We saw some amazing natural wonders, remarkable architecture and charming history, but these aren't the stories we've recounted over and over for the last 20 years. It's been the ordinary and funny stories that helped to grow the relationship between my brother, sister and I that we remember and still tell now.

Stories like me falling over multiple times in the first few days from the horrendous jetlag, or my brother spending a week looking for a pair of tongs only to find that I had dropped them behind his central heating unit when trying to retrieve socks that I'd hung there to dry. Or that one night when we felt like Ben and Jerry's ice cream, so we got rugged up and walked to the local video store together around midnight in freezing conditions to buy a tub of ice cream. We've talked about how my brother had to buy us ski gear at the resort in Andorra because on arrival we found out that we couldn't hire it there and we had no extra money to buy it ourselves, or how my brother's girlfriend broke her leg while skiing and my brother travelled home in the ambulance with her, leaving us to make our own way back to England. I learned that my brother liked weird sci-fi horror movies and screwball comedy and that he was proud of his little sisters when we could answer the Bible history questions at trivia night at the pub. These and many more are the ordinary stories that formed our relationships with one another and that we still talk and laugh about today.

These kinds of ordinary stories are one of many reasons that I love the Bible, God's Word. The Bible is essentially a story about God, filled with ordinary people and their relationship with Him. The Old Testament stories point toward the coming of Jesus, and the New Testament stories tell of His arrival. Every story in the Bible whispers Jesus' name. From the first book to the last, we see God's great plan unfold, to restore a lost and broken humanity to Himself. The Bible came from God, and it points us to Him. It's His great big story and it connects our ordinary story, through our relationship with Jesus, to Him. Isaiah 40:8 says, "The grass withers, the flower fades, but the word of our God will stand forever." The prophet Isaiah used the imagery of withering grass and fading flowers to illustrate the temporary nature of humanity in contrast with the permanence and stability of God and His eternal Word.

The sights, smells, sounds and tastes of England and Europe have faded from my mind but the stories that formed my relationships with my siblings have stood for over 20 years. So it is with this world. While the temporary things from this earth will fade away, the Word of God and His story will last into eternity. Ordinary stories point to extraordinary truths about God. One of the most extraordinary truths about God is that He is the Alpha and the Omega, the beginning and the end (Revelation 21:6). He is eternal, and for that reason His word will last forever. And our ordinary stories find their full meaning and purpose in relationship with Him and His everlasting word.

In the rest of this devotional, you will hear more of the ordinary stories of my life and simple applications that illustrate extraordinary truths about God. You will read some of my favourite memories, my biggest failures and my scariest moments. I'll share some amusing and embarrassing experiences and some of the lessons I've learnt. I hope that as you read these stories, scriptures and prayers, you will see how extraordinary God is and that you might reorient your own story around Him.

The grass withers, the flower fades, but the word of our God will stand forever.
Isaiah 40:8

PRAYER

Thank you, God, for Your Word that stands forever. Thank you that it's Your story and it points to extraordinary truths about You and tells of Your restoration for all humanity. Help me to love Your Word more every day and understand that when my ordinary story is based on the solid rock of Your unfailing Word, my future is eternally secure. Amen.

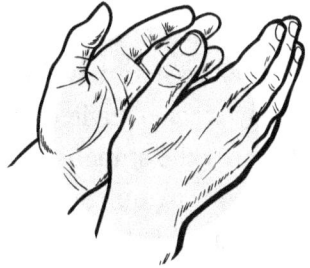

A Father's Applause

Singing isn't a gift of mine. I have always enjoyed singing though and I don't mind thrashing out a tune now and again. The truth is I'm probably tone-deaf and certainly unable to hold a tune or hit any high notes successfully. One of my earliest memories was attending Sunday school with my family at a local church. I loved that everyone was encouraged to sing and no-one seemed to mind whether you sang off-key. Each year, the Sunday school children sang an item at the front of the church. My older sister had a beautiful, sweet singing voice but she was shy and didn't like singing in public. I, however, loved to sing out loud and was confident in front of a crowd. I'd bellow out the words with overzealous, tuneless singing and was young enough to still be considered cute.

When I was in grade eight, I attended a large public high school where it was compulsory to take music as a subject. We learned the guitar in class and for assessment had to sing and play 'Old Time Rock n Roll' by Bob Seger. I was a dedicated student so I practiced hard and managed to pass, but I was by no means a standout performer.

When the school held a music concert that year, the grade eight music students put together an item based on the Bob Seger song we'd practiced in class. My teacher invited me to play the triangle for our performance. Clearly, the student who is asked to play the triangle is the student who wasn't quite up to playing the guitar or singing in a public performance. I cheerfully practiced my part and was feeling super confident that I could successfully nail it.

On the night of the big performance, my dad and older sister took up their places amongst the large audience to watch my debut on the triangle. Minutes before we were about to take the stage, my teacher announced that the lead guitarist and singer could no longer make it due to illness. In a split-second decision, he took the triangle from me, handed me a guitar and gently nudged me out onto the stage, promoting me to star performer. I stood there frozen in fear for a moment, and then did what all good students would do: my best!

At the end of the performance, there was complete silence. I could have heard a pin drop if it wasn't for the pounding of my heart. Then I saw my dad and sister stand up in the audience and start clapping and cheering loudly. Their enthusiasm was contagious and before long the whole audience erupted in applause.

It wasn't an 'Australia's Got Talent' moment where the audience is stunned silent by the sheer brilliance of the performance and then erupts in awe at what they've just witnessed. It was more like a school athletics carnival where the top runners have all finished their race and been handed their ribbons and then the announcer realises that there is still a final runner coming up the last straight. They draw attention to the fact and the spectators all start clapping and cheering, encouraging the runner who isn't ever going to become a star athlete. They receive more applause than the runners who won a place in an attempt to shield them from embarrassment and show them that giving it a go is better than winning. I can tell you with certainty that the loud applause that night was no buffer for the deep embarrassment I felt as I stood there on stage, but it certainly did shield me from feeling alone.

The most special thing that night was whose applause I heard first. In the most embarrassing moment of my life to date, my family stood up and cheered for me. My dad and sister knew that I was meant to be playing the triangle, so their surprise when I came forward into the spotlight was mixed with dismay knowing that this was not only unplanned but also way out of my ability. At the end of what must have felt like an eternity to them, they could have slid down into their seats and pretended they didn't know me. They could have been angry at me afterward for embarrassing them by association, instead, they backed me. They stood up proudly and let me know that they were with me. We laughed about how terrible it was later and enjoyed relating the story to my mum and the rest of my family. We will always have a funny story to tell when we hear Bob Seger's 'Old Time Rock n Roll'.

This story has made me think about God and His character. Sometimes He asks us to do things that are hard or outside our natural ability. Sometimes we end up in situations and circumstances that we would never have chosen, but we can be certain that God will always be with us. Throughout Scripture, He has reassured us that He will never leave us or forsake us. In Joshua 1:9 it says, "Have I not commanded you? Be strong and courageous. Do not be frightened, and do not be dismayed, for the Lord your God is with you wherever you go." Deuteronomy 31:6 says, "Be strong and courageous. Do not fear or be in dread of them, for it is the Lord your God who goes with you. He will not leave you or forsake you." In Matthew's narrative about the birth of Jesus, he writes, "All this took place to fulfil what the Lord had spoken by the Prophet: 'Behold, the virgin shall conceive and bear a son, and they shall call his name Immanuel (which means, God with us)'" (Matthew 1:22-23). And in the final verse of the book of Matthew Jesus says, "I am with you always, to the end of the age" (Matthew 28:20b).

As God's children, we are never alone. When you're in a tight spot and all you can hear is silence, be assured that your heavenly Dad is in the crowd and He's with you. When you're obeying Him and doing your best to do what He has asked of you, you can be sure that the first applause you'll hear is His.

I am with you always, to the end of the age.
Matthew 28:20b

PRAYER

God, you are a good Dad. Thank you that I'm never alone because you are always with me. Your scriptures reassure me of this and my experiences tell me that it's true. While I've felt embarrassment, guilt and shame at times, your presence prevents me from being alone in those moments and that is a wonderful gift. Amen.

Hide and Seek

I grew up as the youngest of four kids. There weren't many things that I was better at than my three older siblings, but there was one thing that I was particularly good at. Given that I was small for my age, and was able to fit into very tight spaces, I was rather good at the game of hide and seek. I could easily hide in various spaces around the house and I would often have to reveal my hiding place when my older sister announced the coveted words, "I give up."

Over the summer holidays, we stayed at my nana and grandad's farm with a number of my cousin's families. We set up our caravan down the paddock, away from the farmhouse. One day, some of my cousins and I decided to play a game of hide and seek. Most of the kids who played were a few years younger than me and one of the youngest was chosen to be 'up'. It's wise when playing hide and seek to set some parameters before the game begins. At the house I grew up in this wasn't necessary because the words, "I give up," could be heard from anywhere in our house. Even if we had stretched the game to include the backyard, there were only about seven meters to the back fence. As we began the game of hide and seek on the farm, we didn't discuss how far the game would extend or which areas would be deemed out of bounds. We also never discussed a time limit or that everyone must be found before the game was over.

In my excitement that I was probably able to outwit and out hide my younger cousins, I ran off in search of the best hiding place. I remembered our family caravan down the paddock and decided to climb into one of the tiny caravan cupboards and shut the door behind me. 'I've nailed it', I thought, 'they'll never find me here'. This was exactly the problem I faced; they never did. Eventually, I realised that no one was going to find me, but when I tried to open the cupboard door, I found that it couldn't be opened from the inside. I tried kicking on it but I was so tightly squashed in there that I didn't have room to move my limbs enough to put any pressure on it. One of my uncles happened to walk past the caravan at the exact moment when I started to panic and scream for help. When he located where the scream was coming from and opened the cupboard, I came tumbling out. I can't remember what actually happened after that but I probably went to find my cousins to make sure they knew I was the real winner!

As an adult, I tend to still be quite good at hiding. Not in cupboards and under beds, but from potential conflict. I'll hide when I've done something wrong, usually by distracting myself or others. I'll fade into the background if things get awkward or uncomfortable. I isolate myself when I'm in trouble rather than turn to others for help and I often hide my true feelings in optimism or just totally dismiss them altogether.

I became aware of this while reading a devotional on Genesis 3. 'And they (Adam and Eve) heard the sound of the Lord God walking in the garden in the cool of the day, and the man and his wife hid themselves from the presence of the Lord God among the trees of the garden' (Genesis 3:8). Adam and Eve had disobeyed God's only command to them and had eaten the fruit from the tree in the middle of the garden. Now they were ashamed, so they hid. In Genesis 3:9 it says, 'But the Lord God called to the man and said to him, "Where are you?"' God didn't ask 'Where are you?' because God didn't know where Adam was. He asked 'Where are you?' because Adam didn't know where he was (Sondergeld, 2022). This wasn't a game of hide and seek; God knew exactly where Adam and Eve were and what they'd done. It was the kindness of God drawing them out of their guilt and shame and towards Himself.

There have been many times when God has asked me, "Where are you?" and I've silently and stubbornly stayed hidden instead of answering God and coming towards Him in all His kindness and mercy. I'm learning that it's better to do what Adam did and answer God and tell Him of my condition. Whatever state I'm in at the time, whether fear, trouble, guilt, shame or discomfort, He is a safe place of refuge. If I'm going to hide then the best hiding place of all is with Him. Next time you feel the temptation to hide or disappear, remember God's question, "Where are you?" Instead of staying silent and hidden, answer Him and His grace will find you no matter what your condition. There is nothing better than being in the presence of the Lord.

> But for me it is good to be near God; I have made the Lord God my refuge, that I may tell of all your works.
>
> Psalm 73:28

PRAYER

Lord, I'm sorry for the times that I've hidden from you in stubborn silence or pride. Thank you for your steadfast love and abundant mercy that finds me whenever I answer you. Thank you that I can draw near to you no matter what my condition. There is no better place to be than in your presence.

Amen.

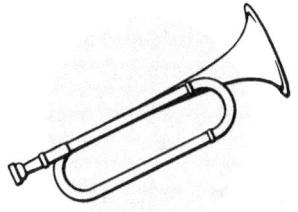

Bugle Bogus

As the youngest sibling of other musical children, I grew up with assumed musical abilities. At primary school, my older brother had shown great potential in music and played both the trombone in the big band and the bugle in the marching band. My sister took private organ lessons and was also successful in becoming a bugler in the school band. I tried playing the organ too, but after one or two lessons my teacher suggested to my mum that this wasn't the instrument for me. When I was old enough to try out for the marching band at school, the teacher just saw my last name and handed me a bugle. I was in! I had made the marching band without having to play one note on the bugle. It seems that the teacher just assumed that because my brother and sister could make a nice sound on the bugle, their skill would run in the family.

The bugle is one of the simplest brass instruments, having no valves or other pitch-altering devices. As such, it is one of the more difficult to play and requires all changes in pitch to be made by varying the shape of the player's mouth (embouchure). I don't know if embouchure, also known as lipping, is something that you're born with skill in or not, but I didn't have the natural ability to get a full, clear tone out of a bugle. I can't remember if I ever asked my older brother or sister to teach me how to play the bugle or not, but I never did learn the bugle call or any of the five notes that make up the bugle scale.

I enjoyed being in the marching band though! I learned how to march in a line, I enjoyed the fancy marching formations and I loved the dapper uniform that I got to wear. I kept my bugle polished and I just pretended to play it whenever I marched in the band. This charade never really presented a problem for me, except every so often at band practice when the teacher would single out one or two people to play on their own. I lived in fear of those practices and the day that I'd get caught out as a bugle bogus. I joke about those days now and I sometimes even brag about the fact that I managed to get through all those years in the marching band without being caught out. But I also remember feeling afraid much of the time and I wonder why I never did tell my teacher that I didn't know how to play the bugle.

As I reflect on this story, I've realised that there have been many other times in my life when I've pretended to be someone I'm not. Sometimes it was to fit in with the crowd, other times it was to make someone else happy, and often it was because I thought it was who others wanted me to be. The problem with being bogus is that it usually leaves you living in fear, and while you're going about pretending to be someone else, you also miss out on the things that you were made to do.

In my final years of primary school, the marching band decided to expand from a drum and bugle corps to include a colour guard. This was a non-musical section of the band that swung coloured flags for a visual effect. Now this would have been my forte! It didn't require any embouchure to swing a flag. It just needed a bit of rhythm and a lot of joy and enthusiasm (of which I was born with bucket loads). My problem was that I was already playing the bugle in the band and so I was ineligible for the colour guard. I might have got myself in on a technicality seeing as I never actually 'played' the bugle, but this would have meant coming clean about being a bugle bogus for the last few years. Way too much time had passed for me to easily own up to the truth. So, I watched on as the high-spirited flag swingers enjoyed their colour guard gig and I continued to pretend to be a bugler.

God doesn't want us to live in fear, missing out on things that He has prepared in advance for us to do. When you walk around pretending to be someone that you're not, you're like someone who is walking around in the dark. Jesus said, "The one who walks in the darkness does not know where he is going" (John 12:35b). If you creep around in the dark you can easily get lost, and you'll usually feel afraid. But when you believe in Jesus and are united to Him you get to walk in the light. Jesus is light and the closer you are to Him, the more honest you will be glad to be. Jesus goes on to say, "While you have the light, believe in the light, that you may become sons of light" (John 12:36).

As a daughter of God who is now walking in the light, I am getting better at being gladly honest. I'm becoming more honest about who I am and the skills and abilities that God has given me. I can own up when I'm being a bogus and God responds to me with kindness and grace. He loves me for who I am, and when I'm walking in that freedom, I can live joyfully swinging a flag rather than pretending to play a bugle.

> If we say we have fellowship with him while we walk in darkness, we lie and do not practice the truth. But if we walk in the light, as he is in the light, we have fellowship with one another, and the blood of Jesus his Son cleanses us from all sin.
>
> 1 John 1:6-7

PRAYER

Oh God of light, in you there is no darkness at all. The closer I get to you I find more and more light. Thank you that your light shows me more of who I am and I can see where I'm going and be confident of the things that you have for me to do. Help me to stay connected to you, Jesus, so that I don't end up stumbling around fearfully in the dark. And when I do find myself in darkness and fear, lead me quickly back to the light where I can be honest again. Amen.

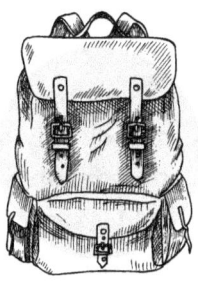

Bag Carrier

I grew up as the baby in my family. I was literally introduced that way, and I owned that title so much that I had to intentionally learn to stop talking like a baby once it was no longer considered cute. Sometimes children born as the youngest in their family are driven to become independent and long to be seen as autonomous in their own right. This was definitely not the case for me. I not only owned that title and place in our family, but I made a habit of profiting from being needy and dependent on others.

When I was in late primary school, my sister and I would walk home from school each day as we lived less than a block away. I dreaded the last day of each term when we would take our school books home for the holidays. My books would add a considerable weight to my school bag, which I then had to carry home on my back. By the time I reached sixth grade, I had gained the attention of a boy who lived not far from our house. He walked the same path home as I did and I decided to make use of him. On one of those end-of-term days when my bag was too heavy to skip home happily after school, I asked this boy if he would carry my bag for me. He was thrilled at the chance to impress me and show he was strong enough to not only carry his heavy bag but mine as well, so he willingly obliged.

This soon became the norm, not only on the last day of term but on any day that he happened to catch up with me at the gate and offer his bag-carrying services. My older sister was mortified that I would depend on a boy to do such a task. She took great pride in being able to carry her bag no matter how heavy it was. The next year, she went off to high school, so I was able to utilise the services of my bag carrier every day without remark.

By the time I was in grade 10, my dependent attitude hadn't changed much. I arranged for boys to send me an easy pass of the ball on the basketball court or the soccer field and sailed my way to a pass in PE. When we went on a survival camp and had to carry our share of the cooking utensils and food on an overnight hike, I found some boys who jumped at the challenge of a heavier pack. I passed out the contents of my backpack until it was light enough for me to walk and chat easily without losing my breath.

As I've sat in Christian small groups over the years, I've often heard people speak about their "independent streak" as a negative and how they desire to be more dependent. I've listened thinking, "I can't relate to that at all; I'm nailing the whole dependent thing!" However, being largely dependent on other people comes with its own set of problems. As I've grown into adulthood, I've sometimes found it hard to make even simple decisions on my own. I've been so quick to ask for help in times past that I find it hard to problem-solve when no one is around for advice. While I'm very grateful for the support of people around me, human strength and wisdom are limited and can only help so much. My dependence has kept me immature in my faith in God and I've come to realise that neither independence nor dependence is godly in itself. It is dependence on God that helps you to grow up in him and build a mature faith.

In Psalm 121 it says, "I lift up my eyes to the hills. From where does my help come? My help comes from The Lord, who made heaven and earth." When I turn to God for my help, He is infinitely resourceful and able to provide what I need. He made me and He knows me and all my deepest longings and truest needs. In His boundless wisdom, He can give me the insight, understanding and strength to carry out a task. He can also grow and strengthen me through those experiences. Psalm 121 goes on to say that God is my keeper and He will not slumber nor sleep. There have been times in my life when there has been no one on this earth that I could turn to for help in my hour of need. It's been so comforting to know that the perfectly loving and all-powerful God is available 24/7.

Though we are meant to live in family and community and be able to rely on one another for support, I've learned the richness of lifting my eyes and depending on the only One who knows me fully. I'm not just the baby of my family anymore, now I can own the title of being God's child too. I have a place in His family and He welcomes me to be needy and dependent on Him – the maker of heaven and earth!

I lift up my eyes to the hills. From where does my help come? My help comes from the Lord, who made heaven and earth.

Psalm 121:1-2

PRAYER

Lord God, maker of heaven and earth, help me to lift my eyes to you for help. You are infinitely resourceful to help in times of trouble. You are boundless in wisdom and perfect in love. You are my keeper and you never slumber or sleep, but are ever present and available. You welcome me as your child and invite me to be dependent on You. Oh, what freedom and peace there is in that. Amen.

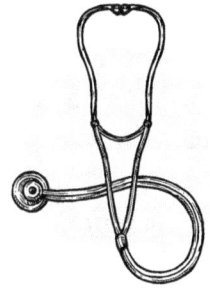

Sickness Benefits

When I was nine years old, I spent a school term in and out of hospital. I just woke up one morning and couldn't walk on my left ankle. I remember crawling down the hallway to my parent's room to tell them. They were pretty relaxed about it at first, thinking that maybe I had bugle band practice that day and was looking for a reason to get out of school. After determining that I truly wasn't able to hold any weight on my ankle, my dad concluded that I must have been sleep-walking during the night and somehow sprained it. I did get out of bugle band practice that day as dad carried me in to see the doctor who then hospitalised me for further testing.

In the following days and weeks, I had similar joint-related symptoms in other areas of my body including my wrist and elbow. I was finally diagnosed with a form of arthritis called Reiter's Syndrome which is uncommon in young girls. Over the next few months, I had lots of medical interventions; surgery to take fluid from my ankle, regular blood tests, half plaster casts for my legs, and the use of a wheelchair and walking frame.

I was then diagnosed with Iritis, a condition of the eye, which is common in patients with Reiter's Syndrome. This resulted in a week spent in a dark hospital room having eye drops administered, initially every half hour. I had to wear sunglasses whenever I went out into the sun and I had regular appointments at the Ophthalmologist and the Paediatrician. While I was in hospital, I had a cannula to make it easier for the nurses to administer my many medications. As much as I tried, I just couldn't swallow a tablet and the nurses were tired of hiding them in my mashed potato.

Apart from learning a lot about the workings of medical waiting rooms and the children's ward at the hospital, I also learned a lot about my family and friends during that time. I learned that my mum was really capable, kind and able to juggle whatever balls were thrown at her. She managed everything that was going on at home with my three older siblings and she even made a hospital diary for me, recording all the daily occurrences. During the weeks that I was able to come home from the hospital, she not only took care of everything but became an expert at mixing tablets with honey to help them go down.

I learned that my dad was good at being there. He would turn up at the hospital on his way to and from work. On his days off, he'd show up and watch movies with me to help pass the time. I learned that my oldest sister's way of caring for me was to write me letters. She would ask her friends for their favourite jokes and would write them out to cheer me up. My other sister visited me the most with mum or dad and would fill me in on everything that I was missing out on while in the hospital. Even though she was quiet and shy at school, she went out of her comfort zone to pass on information to my friends and teachers about how I was doing. My older brother got his learner's licence while I was sick and was super proud to come and pick me up from the hospital and drive me home. I also learned that there are other sickness benefits for those in the hospital; I received lots of 'get well soon' cards and gifts.

Upon returning to school, I continued to wear the half-plaster casts on my legs during class, wear sunglasses in the sun and lean on the walking frame during recess time. I learned that some of the girls that I thought were good friends, weren't very nice at all. While other girls that I hadn't given much time to were actually kind and didn't care about the things that made me a bit weird. Now that I look back, I realise that I saw so many things about other people that I might not have seen if I hadn't gone through that time of sickness.

What I wanted most through that time though, was a comforting presence that never left me. My parents were unable to stay with me overnight while I was in hospital and I remember feeling afraid and lonely after they left for home each night. And upon my return to school, I longed for a constant friend who understood me.

This is what is so special about my faith in Jesus. When I experience sickness or injury, it forces me to slow down and see things differently. When life gets disrupted by sickness, I tend to become more aware of God and who He is. I see His tender mercies more easily and I notice how He takes care of me in the small things. Psalm 23 speaks of the Lord as a shepherd; someone who guides, directs and tends to His sheep. When I read Psalm 23, I can't help but slow down and read it carefully, as if it's meant to be read that way. It starts with, "The Lord is my shepherd; I shall not want. He makes me lie down in green pastures. He leads me beside still waters. He restores my soul. He leads me in paths of righteousness for his name's sake" (Psalm 23:1-3).

When I'm sick, I feel weak and in need of a good Shepherd. I need someone to lovingly lead me, guide me and tend to my needs. As I follow The Good Shepherd, Jesus, I find more than I could hope for. "Even though I walk through the valley of the shadow of death, I will fear no evil, for you are with me; your rod and your staff, they comfort me" (Psalm 23:4). When sickness forces me to stop and I choose to find my rest in God, I receive His sickness benefits – peace and comfort, goodness and mercy, and most of all His presence. A comforting presence that will never leave me and a constant friend who understands me.

The Lord is my shepherd; I shall not want. Psalm 23:1

PRAYER

Thank you Lord for times of good health and healing, and also for the times when I'm sick or weak. These times are a blessing because they force me to stop or slow down and see things that I might not otherwise get to see. Thank you that you are a good shepherd. Help me to trust that you will lead, guide and tend to my needs. Let me know your peace, comfort and mercy in whatever circumstances I face. Amen.

Glow Worm

For most of my life I've been scared of the dark. To be honest, I've been scared of a lot of other things too, and all of those things seem scarier in the dark. Up until about the age of 14, I shared a bedroom with my sister and every night as we'd go to sleep, we'd argue about the light. I wanted to sleep with the lamp on and the door open, and she loved to sleep in absolute darkness with the door closed to shut out any noise. We had bunk beds, and because she was 18 months older than me, she slept on the top. I spent my childhood being envious of her top bunk but I learned that having the bottom bed did have its advantages too.

Each night I'd turn the lamp on, open the door and climb easily into bed. She would then climb down the ladder, turn the lamp off and close the door. Just as she'd settle back into her top bunk, I'd jump up, turn the lamp back on and open the door. We'd do this several times and then she'd give up and throw a shirt over her eyes to try and block out the light. After playing this game for a while, my sister eventually kept a cane stick up in her bed so that she could lean over and push the door shut without having to get up. I was very persistent though and would just continue to jump up and open the door as many times as it took to have it open as I fell asleep.

One birthday, my mum gave me a glow worm. It was a small, hollow plastic toy in the shape of a cute worm with a hole at the bottom. It was designed to sit on a lamp for a few minutes and then emit a slight glow in the dark for a few hours before fading out completely. I loved my little glow worm but it didn't quite give enough light for me to feel secure without the lamp on. One night, after playing the same nightly games with my sister, I wondered whether my glow worm might get extra bright if I left it on the lamp for extra time. I decided to give it a try and planned to leave it for half an hour, but I fell asleep with the plastic worm sitting on the hot lamp bulb. It did get extra bright that night but it also got really hot and started to burn.

My dad worked odd shifts at this time which meant that some nights he would get home from work after we'd already gone to sleep. He was a man of routine, so each night that he worked late he would come into our room and give us a kiss goodnight. I'd try really hard to stay awake so I could see him, but I hardly ever did. One night I did manage to stay awake but I pretended to be asleep. Right as he kissed my cheek, I opened my eyes wide and said, "Boo!" It gave him the fright of his life. So did the night of the burning glow worm!

That night was one of those late shifts for my dad and as he came into our bedroom, he smelt smoke and burning plastic and discovered my glow worm burning so brightly that it had charred the bottom completely black. If it had been left any longer, it would probably have started a fire. The irony is that while I was actually quite safe in my dark room with my sister sleeping above me and my dad watching over me, my fear of the dark had led to my sister and I being in actual danger.

Fears and anxieties are very common, even among God's children. King David, called a man after God's own heart in the Bible, wrote about fear in many of his Psalms. In Psalm 3, David cries out to God to save him from enemies that were rising against him. King David did have real enemies of which he was afraid, but he also had anxieties that stopped him from sleeping at night. He was worried about what people thought of him and what they were saying about him (Psalm 3:2). In verse 3, he reminds himself of who God is and says, "But you, O Lord, are a shield about me, my glory and the lifter of my head." He states his confidence in the Lord amidst his danger, fears and complaints. He acknowledges that God can lift his head even in his state of sin and shame and look upon him with love and grace. In verse 5, King David goes on to say, "I lay down and slept; I woke again, for the Lord sustained me," as a declaration of his trust in the Lord for his safety and protection.

In recent years, I've learned to follow King David's example amid my own fears and anxieties, both when I've feared a physical threat and also when I've been fearful of something that attacks my sense of who I am; my identity. This worry about threats to our identity is often the most common and debilitating type of fear that we face and is called anxiety. Tim Keller speaks about this in his sermon, Praying Our Fears. He says that the first word in Psalm 3:3 is very important, "but." This implies, I'm scared and afraid, but I'm going to do something (Keller, 2000). What does King David do? He remembers that God is a shield around him. He then humbly allows God to be the lifter of his head.

When I am fearful, I try to remember that God's protection is a shield about me and that God, in all His power, is for me and with me. I can then humbly repent of my need for other people's approval and settle into my place as God's child, whom He loves and approves and calls to do His good work. When I do this, I don't need to try and make myself glow more brightly to feel safe and secure. I can rest in the glow of God's protection, grace and love.

> But you, O Lord, are a shield about me, my glory and the lifter of my head. Psalm 3:3
>
> **PRAYER**
>
> Thank you Lord, that you are my shield of protection. You take me and surround me with yourself. Your glory covers me continually and you lift my head high when I bow before you in my sin and shame. Help me to cry out to you for help and to allow you to strengthen and sustain me so that I may live, not in fear, but in the power of your great love. Amen.

Night Sky

One of my fondest childhood memories is that of visiting Nana and Grandad's farm. They lived about an hour away and we would often go there for a day trip on the weekend. The farm was a beautiful place with a flowing creek and a backdrop of hills and rock faces. As much as I loved spending the days there, I also loved the car trip home.

As a child, I would rarely be out at night time, so driving home in the dark under a starlit sky, away from city lights, was a special experience for me. We had a car with five seats for our family of six, so all four of the kids would be packed into the backseat for the car trip. My brother was a teen by this time and had really long legs, so my sister and I would share the middle seat belt and my brother would stretch his long legs out across both of our laps. Somehow, despite being squished, I'd settle in and look out the window on those trips home and I would always have the same thought…

I'd think about how small and insignificant I felt compared to the vast night sky. Then I'd think about my life and imagine that I must be part of a bigger story. A story in which my life was not just like a play, with an opening curtain at the beginning and a closing curtain at the end, but rather a small part of something greater. Each time that we would travel home at night on those roads, I would look up and know in my heart that God was real. I was sure that He was with me and that my life was part of His great big story. The fact that I knew this as a child by simply looking up at the stars from a squashy car seat is a testimony to God's wonderful works.

This certainty about God was still true for me years later when that same Grandad I'd visited as a child was at the end of a long battle with cancer. Grandad was a happy, gentle man with a broad smile, a balding head and huge ear lobes. I remember rubbing Vaseline ointment into his dry head and pulling on his big soft ears. He was grateful, rarely complained, and after every meal or special occasion he would say, "Well we've all done very well." He loved his chickens and cows, and every time another calf was born, he'd name it after one of his grandchildren. When I was sick and in hospital, he came to visit me with the exciting news that he had named his new calf Renee. I remember him being patient, humble, loving and generous with what he had.

We went to visit him just before he passed away at 69 years old. He was smiling and he looked so peaceful, so I asked him how he could be content when he knew that he was going to die. He told me that he was sure that he would soon be in Heaven with Jesus. I was 14 years old at the time and hadn't been to church for many years, but that night, I went home and found a Good News Bible that I had been given at Sunday school. I opened it up to the New Testament and started reading. As I sat in my room that night, I decided to ask God to forgive my sins and to help me follow Jesus. That was the night that I became a Christian and I remember feeling such unexplainable peace. Grandad died soon after and it was a really sad time for my family, but I found peace in knowing that he was no longer in any pain and was smiling his big smile up in Heaven. I found hope in God through that difficult time and His comfort and peace stayed with me from that night on.

Psalm 139:5 says, "You hem me in, behind and before, and lay your hand upon me." I believed this truth in a small way as a child looking up at the night sky from a squished back car seat. I knew it more when my beloved Grandad died soon after I became a Christian. I know it in an even deeper way today. Psalm 139 speaks of the greatness of God and how He knows all and is everywhere. But the best part is that He doesn't just know all… He knows me, is everywhere with me and created me. He places a hedge of protection around me and His gracious hand directs me with love and care.

The same is true for you! God is present everywhere and He is personal. When we are confident in the love and care of God our Father, His constant knowledge of us is a comfort. Grandad's life was in God's hands, as is mine, and it always has been. God is with us; He knows our thoughts and He directs our paths. Our life isn't just like a play with an opening curtain at the beginning and a closing curtain at the end but rather a small part of a much bigger story that lasts forever!

You hem me in, behind and before, and lay your hand upon me. Psalm 139:5

PRAYER

Father, thank you for always being with me. Thank you that I can see you and know you through the vast night sky. Thank you that you have continued to hem me in, behind and before, as you love and care for me. Help me to know this to be true and to find such knowledge a comfort every day. Amen.

Top Dog

I learned to water-ski when I was in high school. I loved the feeling of getting up on the skis and gliding across a dam while holding onto a rope attached to the back of a boat. Family friends of ours owned a boat and we would go skiing with them whenever they went out. This was a little too infrequent for my teenage love of water-skiing, so I asked my dad whether we could buy our own boat. I told him I would invest five hundred dollars into the boat if he could put in the rest. My dad liked the idea and started looking for a second-hand ski boat. We found one for sale with an outboard motor powerful enough to pull a couple of skiers, and true to my word, I contributed five hundred dollars towards the purchase.

The boat had 'Top Dog' painted up the side, so from that day on it was simply known as Top Dog. My dad then bought all the gear that we would need to go water-skiing, including two sets of skis, ropes, life jackets, wet suit pants, and a heap of other boating equipment. For Top Dog's first water-skiing trip, my dad paid for the fuel that we would need to spend the day out on the water and bought the permit to ski on the dam. The whole setup was quite costly and probably outweighed my share of five hundred dollars by more than ten to one.

When we arrived at the dam for Top Dog's maiden voyage, my dad announced that since I was part owner of the boat, I could have the first ski. From then on, he always referred to Top Dog as 'our' boat and always insisted that I had special owner privileges such as getting the first ski on every trip; anyone would have thought that we were equal partners in ownership of the boat. Top Dog was a great boat and we enjoyed many hours skiing behind her.

She might have been a Top Dog, but she was also an 'old dog'. On occasion, we would arrive at the dam, get the boat into the water, and find that she simply wouldn't go. It was my dad who paid all the mechanical bills to get her going again. He never once asked me to contribute to the maintenance costs but continued to call it our boat and treat me like a joint owner. Top Dog certainly belonged to my dad but he chose to generously include me in the ownership title anyway.

My dad's generosity reminds me of one of my favorite parables in the Bible; the parable of the generous master, found in Matthew 20:1-16. Jesus tells the story of a master who goes out early, at about six o'clock in the morning, to hire laborers for his vineyard. He agrees with the laborers to pay them a denarius (a day's wage at the time) for a day's work. Throughout the day he hires more laborers who are standing idle in the marketplace because no one else has hired them. He hires some at nine o'clock, more at twelve, more again at three in the afternoon, and even some at about five o'clock. These final laborers only work for one hour before sunset. At the end of the day, the owner of the vineyard asks his foreman to pay the laborers their wages, beginning with the last hired, up to the first. They are all paid the same amount (a denarius), despite the different number of hours worked. Not unexpectedly, those hired first complain to the master that though they worked a whole day in the heat, they earned no more money than those who started late in the day. "But he replied to one of them, Friend, I am doing you no wrong. Did you not agree with me for a denarius? Take what belongs to you and go. I choose to give to this last worker as I give to you. Am I not allowed to do what I choose with what belongs to me? Or do you begrudge my generosity?" (Matthew 20:13-15).

This parable is not about business practices but rather about God's generosity in the kingdom of heaven. God can do what He chooses with what belongs to Him, and our response should be one of glad thankfulness for His generosity. Jesus goes on to say, "So the last will be first, and the first last" (Matthew 20:16). He also finishes the parable directly before this one with the same saying (Matthew 19:30). The owner does something unexpected because he is a generous master. He honours the workers hired last by paying them first, and he lavishly rewards them by paying them twelve times what they probably deserved and expected to be paid.

God is a lot like this master. He is generous and honours and rewards those whom He chooses. He is loving, just, and gracious, and our entry into His kingdom is not gained by our work or action, but by His generosity. We do very little, while He does everything, to secure our place in His kingdom forever. Ephesians 2:8 says, "For by grace you have been saved through faith. And this is not your own doing; it is the gift of God." It's like me giving a measly five hundred dollars towards a water-skiing boat and being given the title of owner because the true owner, who paid for everything, chose to honour me for my meagre share.

Am I not allowed to do what I choose with what belongs to me? Or do you begrudge my generosity? So the last will be first, and the first last. Matthew 20:15-16

PRAYER

Thank you, Lord, that you are a good and generous master. You choose to honour me and lavish me with the reward of an eternal place in your kingdom. You choose to do this even though I do very little for you and you do everything in return. Help me to offer up a humble and cheerful attitude in my service to you and to be thankful and glad for your generosity to me. Amen.

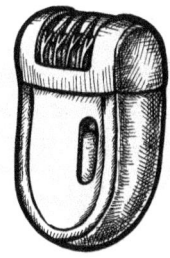

Lady Shave

In December of 1998, I was preparing for my first overseas holiday. I had signed up for my school's 'G'day USA' trip. When I heard about the trip, I was desperate to be a part of it as we would experience an American school in Seattle and then go to Disneyland, Universal Studios and Knott's Berry Farm (a theme park) in California. I had money saved from my work at Hungry Jacks, so my parents said that I could go as long as my sister went too.

I decided to pack my battery-operated 'Lady Shave' for the trip, an electric razor that I owned. I loved my pink Lady Shave as I could shave my legs anywhere, even in the car on the way to school. I threw it into my toiletry bag, batteries and all, and packed it into my checked luggage for the USA. We said goodbye to our family, and then my sister and I, along with our classmates boarded our plane to Sydney, and then on to San Francisco. After spending three wonderful weeks traveling around the West Coast of America, we arrived at the Los Angeles International Airport (LAX) to fly back home to Australia.

Even in January of 1999, LAX airport was already one of the world's largest and busiest airports. This was more than two years before the 9/11 terrorist attacks and security was more relaxed compared to what it was afterwards. Checked luggage wasn't as highly scrutinized as it is post 9/11, but they still had checks in place if anything seemed suspicious and we were still required to sign a declaration that we had packed our bags and weren't carrying anything illegal or harmful.

I couldn't fit my toiletry bag into my tightly packed suitcase after three weeks of travel. So, unbeknownst to my sister, I unzipped her bag and squashed my toiletries in while we were waiting in line to go through security. When it was my sister's turn to check her bag, several security guards came rushing over to where we were standing. One of the men grabbed her suitcase and the rest of them formed a circle around it. They then started to move backward away from the suitcase, ensuring the crowds were kept a safe distance away. When asked whose suitcase it was, my sister admitted it was hers and assured them that she had packed it herself.

As I looked over at her suitcase, I saw what had made it seem suspicious; it was gently vibrating. I suddenly had the realisation that my Lady Shave must have switched on when I had squashed my toiletry bag into her suitcase. I tried to get her attention and tell her what I had done, but she was too mortified by what was happening to listen. The security guard in the middle of the circle opened her suitcase with one quick, brave move and swiftly located where the vibration was coming from. He picked up my toiletry bag, opened it, and pulled out the pink Lady Shave. He flicked the switch off and the danger was over. The security guard looked quite embarrassed as he stood there holding the electric shaver, but not nearly as embarrassed as my poor sister who was left to pick up her belongings. I apologised profusely to her, but she was pretty angry with me and took a while to see the funny side of the situation. She did eventually enjoy retelling that story to our family and friends upon our return to Australia.

This story makes me think about misunderstandings and being misunderstood. There have been plenty of times in my life when I've felt misunderstood; where something I've said has been taken out of context, where my motives or actions have been misjudged or misinterpreted, or when who I am is not how someone else has perceived me. Sometimes I have contributed to these misunderstandings by not communicating clearly. Other times misunderstandings are caused when I'm unable to see my motivations and actions purely. When this is the case, I've had to humbly confess and acknowledge that I've done something wrong. Even if there are parts of a situation where I feel that my words or actions were justified, there are often parts where I need to make an effort to clear up any wrongdoings on my part. While I never meant or expected my Lady Shave to be perceived as a threatening bomb in my sister's suitcase, I should have asked her permission before putting it in there.

Jesus was the most misunderstood person in the Bible. He was misunderstood by those closest to him, including his disciples, and his mission and motives were completely misinterpreted by his enemies. Because Jesus understands being misunderstood, we can run to him when we feel similarly. Our peace doesn't rest in the perceptions of others, but rather in the presence of our good Lord who knows and understands us perfectly. Psalm 139:1-3 says, "O Lord, you have searched me and known me! You know when I sit down and when I rise up; you discern my thoughts from afar. You search out my path and my lying down and are acquainted with all my ways." Focusing on God and how He knows everything about me, replaces my longing for 'understanding' from the world. Even when my Lady Shave is perceived as a bomb threat in LAX airport, I can be confident that God knew my heart's true motives. We can rest in the truth that we are wholly understood by God.

O Lord, you have searched me and known me! You know when I sit down and when I rise up; you discern my thoughts from afar. You search out my path and my lying down and are acquainted with all my ways. Psalm 139:1-3

PRAYER

Thank you, God, for intimately understanding me. You know me, my thoughts and my ways perfectly and I can be confident in being wholly understood by you. Thank you that I can come to you for help and forgiveness when I have done the wrong thing and contributed to misunderstandings. Help me to face these situations with courage and humility and then look to you for your loving understanding. Amen.

Mail Box

I lived in the same house from birth until when I got married. All of my childhood memories and stories of home happened in that one house. There were six people in my family, and we all lived in a four-bedroom house with one bathroom and one toilet. There was often a wait for the toilet, made lengthier because my mum would hang laminated poems, stories, and fun facts on the toilet walls. The reading material grew over time, which increased the length of the average toilet trip.

One of the posters that I must have read hundreds of times throughout my childhood was called 'Rules to a Happy Home'. One of the rules said, "Smile – it takes 72 muscles to frown and only 14 to smile." Smiling and laughter were encouraged in our house. As the proverb says, "A joyful heart is good medicine, but a crushed spirit dries up the bones" (Proverbs 17:22). I remember laughing a lot while growing up with my siblings. There are many stories that we still re-tell together with so much laughter that we can hardly get the words out.

One of these is the mailbox story. When I got my learner driver's license at age 16 and a half, my older sister thought that she was an eligible supervisor. One day as we were going out together, she suggested that I drive. I was so stoked that she trusted me enough to drive that I readily jumped behind the wheel of her car. Our driveway came up from the road as a single lane until the mailbox and then split off into two separate parking spaces. One parking space was straight ahead in the carport and the other one angled off to the right. I started to reverse the car out of the angled parking space but misjudged when I should have started turning the car to reverse it back down the single lane to the road. Instead of turning down the driveway and onto the road, I reversed straight back into our mailbox. It was a small, steel box on a thin, steel post, so when I hit it, the post bent over and snapped off at the base.

For whatever reason, this accident made my sister and I laugh. We both have the tendency to laugh when we're nervous or experiencing overwhelming emotions and that day we laughed really hard! When we finally stopped laughing, I got out of the car, picked up the broken letterbox, and stuck it back into the ground. You couldn't really tell that anything had happened except that it was about 10cm shorter than it had been before. My sister decided it wasn't a great idea to let me drive anymore, so she resumed the driver's seat and we headed off to wherever we were going together.

That night at the dinner table, my dad told us that the weirdest thing had happened to him when he got home after work. He went on to say that as he went to get the mail out of the mailbox, it just completely fell over. My sister and I couldn't contain our laughter, which made my mum and dad laugh too. When the laughter died down and we could finally speak again, we did tell them the truth about what had happened to the mailbox. That weekend my dad cemented the mailbox back into the ground. He also firmly took back the supervisor's responsibilities for my learner permit and I didn't drive with my sister again until I had passed my driving test.

Laughter is mentioned many times in both the Old and New Testaments of the Bible. Ecclesiastes 3:4 says, "A time to weep, and a time to laugh; a time to mourn, and a time to dance." The Bible is clear that there is a time for us to laugh. Laughter is a physical sign of the inward working of joy in the Lord. One of my favourite Bible stories is about laughter. It's the story of the elderly Sarah (the wife of Abraham) who found out that she would have a baby. She had longed to have a baby and had tried to control circumstances to force this to happen in her way and timing. When the Lord brought about His plan in His timing, Sarah laughed. Genesis 21:6 says, 'And Sarah said, "God has made laughter for me; everyone who hears will laugh over me."' Her laughter was a symbol of her victory and awe at the good and amazing things that God had done. This is why Sarah named her baby Isaac, which means 'one who laughs.'

I hadn't thought about just how good and healthy it is to laugh regularly until a friend of mine sent me an encouraging text message that simply said, "I'm praying for laughter for you this week." My friend wanted me to find joy in laughter and God wants that for us too. Have you laughed today? If not, ask the Lord to fill you with His joy and give you the sweet gift and blessing of laughter. Why? Because a joyful heart is good medicine, and it takes 72 muscles to frown but only 14 to smile.

And Sarah said, "God has made laughter for me; everyone who hears will laugh over me."
Genesis 21:6.

PRAYER

Thank you, Lord, for the sweet gift and blessing of laughter. It is a sign of the inward working of joy and a symbol of victory and awe at the good things You have done. Help me to laugh, like Sarah did, at the wondrous ways that You are at work in my life and in the lives of those around me. Amen.

Hungry Jacks Origins

My first job was working at our local Hungry Jacks. I was fourteen and nine months old, and though it wasn't the first time I had worked, it was the first time that I was employed by someone other than my dad. It was also the first time that I was paid more than five dollars an hour. I worked there alongside my sister and a bunch of really great boys. Some of these boys invited me and my sister to their church, which was just around the corner from our house. My sister went along with them, and I finally started going with her when I was about sixteen and a half and could no longer think of a reason not to.

During that time, I also made friends with another boy at Hungry Jacks called Nath. He went to a different church, but I found out that his nana went to the same little local church as me. I would chat with him about anything and everything whenever we worked the same shift, and we started hanging out together outside of work with a few of our Hungry Jacks friends. When he finished grade 12, Nath enrolled in our local university to study primary teaching. I had already been at uni for one year at this stage, so he used this fact to his advantage and invited me to his house to help him with his enrolment.

Upon arriving at his house, I found that his parents were out of town and he was cooking dinner for himself, his brother and his best mate that night. They invited me to stay for dinner and I thought, why not? I sat down at the table to eat a beautifully prepared dish of apricot chicken with them, impressed not only by his culinary skills but also by the way he had skilfully worked a dinner date into the uni enrolment invitation. Halfway through dinner, Nath's mate announced that the chicken was still raw. The boys pushed their plates away and started looking for two-minute noodle packets in the cupboard to replace the ruined dinner. At that moment, Nath looked at my plate and simultaneously realised that not only was I a very fast eater, but I had politely eaten all of the raw chicken on my plate. I already liked him too much to make him feel discouraged after all the effort he had made to cook for me. That night sealed the deal for us. I never did end up with food poisoning and we started seeing each other most days for the next four years until our wedding.

On the eve of our wedding, we invited our parents and bridal party to join us for dinner at Hungry Jacks. Our party included Nath's brother and best mate who had been with us on that first dinner date of raw apricot chicken, my sister who had worked alongside us at Hungry Jacks, and other special family and friends. After we were married and had kids, we decided that it would be a fun anniversary tradition to go to Hungry Jacks and reminisce about how we first met. One year on our anniversary, when our eldest daughter was around eight years old, she told us how much she enjoyed this tradition, but also how glad she was that we didn't meet at the dentist!

I love traditions that celebrate the beginning of something important. Hungry Jacks is a reminder to me that God directed my life and provided for me. He used that little part-time job to provide a local church for me to grow in my faith and a boy for me to grow to love and journey through life with. These things are worth remembering, celebrating and thanking God for. As a follower of Jesus, God promises to direct our steps and care for every detail of our lives. The book of Proverbs gives wisdom about the fact that we can make whatever plans we like, but it's the Lord who determines our steps (Proverbs 16:9). When you place your trust in a good and loving God who is also powerful and just, you can trust Him to work all things out for good.

Often, we don't have the advantage of seeing the path ahead, and so we can tend to veer off and stumble along the way. Even so, we can be assured that God holds us by the hand. As we continue to submit our plans and purposes to Him, He will make our paths straight. I committed my life to Jesus at the age of 14, but over the next few years, I stumbled in my young faith. All the while, God was holding my hand, directing my steps and caring about the details of my life as they unfolded. He was there as I started work at Hungry Jacks, as I began attending church, and certainly as I ate raw apricot chicken. Commit your plans to Him too and trust that the good Lord's purposes will prevail.

The steps of a man are established by the Lord, when he delights in his way; though he fall, he shall not be cast headlong, for the Lord upholds his hand.
Psalm 37:23-24

PRAYER

Thank you Lord for directing my steps and holding my hand, even when I'm veering off the path or stumbling along. Help me to submit my plans to you and trust in you as you determine my steps. Amen.

The Proposal

The night that Nath proposed to me is etched in my mind as a special moment that captured my heart and memory forever. It was a Tuesday night because we had always reserved Tuesday nights for date night. There was a marketing campaign at the time called "Cheap Tuesday" where businesses gave discounts on Tuesdays for the cinema, video and DVD hire, take away and restaurants. As we were cash-poor university students, Nath and I took full advantage of those discounts on our date nights for many years.

On this particular Tuesday date night, Nath picked me up in his car, blindfolded me and drove me to the fuel station. Either it hadn't occurred to him to get fuel before this momentous occasion, or it was part of his plan to confuse me so I didn't know where we were headed or guess that this might be "the Date" where he would ask me to marry him. Regardless of his intentions, I was so distracted and embarrassed by what people might think if they saw me blindfolded at the fuel station to even think about what might lie ahead. Once we were fuelled up, Nath drove around the back streets of Toowoomba for a while so that I was completely lost. Eventually, we pulled up somewhere and he asked me to stay in the car for a minute so that he could set something up. Again, I was concerned about whether it was safe for me to be blindfolded in a parked car not knowing where I was or what he was doing. Thankfully, I had learned over our three-and-a-half years of dating that there was usually some method in his madness and romance in his randomness.

When Nath finally returned to the car, he led me inside what felt like a big quiet building and asked me to sit down on a seat. A few minutes later he asked me to take off my blindfold and revealed that I was sitting on a red velvet couch in the middle of our church auditorium. It was the only chair in the whole room and he was sitting on a stool on the stage with guitar in hand, a microphone in front of him and a spotlight shining on his beaming face. He announced that this was a concert just for me and began to sing a song that he had written. It was about us and it made me laugh out loud. It was funny and quirky and then turned raw and emotional and made me cry. When the song was finished, he walked across the room to me, got down on one knee and asked me to be his wife.

What happened next continues to baffle him to this day, but we've both come to laugh about it. My mind has always been able to think about multiple things at once but unfortunately it doesn't always prioritise the order in which they come out of my mouth. So, while I was thinking a resounding 'yes' to his proposal, I was also wondering how all the other chairs had been removed from the building and who would have to put them back before church on Sunday. Before I said yes aloud, I asked, "Do we need to put all of the chair's back?" He was confused by my question but answered by telling me that he had organised his best mate to put them all back the next day. Once my concern about the chairs was satisfied, I said yes to his proposal and he proceeded to put a petite diamond ring on my finger. It was a special night indeed.

As I've thought about Nath's proposal all these years later, it is only now that I fully appreciate the detail of that night. There was such significance in Nath removing all the chairs and leaving only a single couch in the middle of a huge auditorium. He wanted me to know that I was worth the effort of my own personal concert. He wanted me to know that I was incredibly valuable to him.

When I consider Nath's demonstration of extravagant love for me in his proposal, my thoughts turn to God and an amazing verse in Zephaniah 3. In verse 17, God says that He will take great delight in us and will rejoice over us with singing. Whenever I think about God rejoicing over me, I think about me being the only person in the room. I think about how God would choose to rejoice and sing over me even if I was the only person present. That's how valuable I am to Him, and so are you. He knows all of your flaws and failures and still chooses to sing over you. He knows everything about you and takes great delight in you. You don't need to question whether you need to put all the chairs back. You simply need to say yes to Him.

The Lord your God is in your midst, a mighty one who will save; he will rejoice over you with gladness; he will quiet you by his love; he will exult over you with loud singing. Zephaniah 3:17

PRAYER

God, thank you that you are with me and you take great delight in me. Thank you that I am valuable to you and so significant that you rejoice over me with singing. You have chosen me and I am fully approved and accepted by You, the Mighty Warrior who saves. Help me to live out my identity in Christ - Your Beloved!
Amen.

New Lenses

I've worn glasses for short sightedness since primary school. Well, at least I owned glasses back then; I'm not sure I ever actually wore them. They spent more time in my school bag than on my face. In the nineties, glasses weren't the fashion accessory they are now. Terms like 'four eyes' were floating around and attaching themselves to anyone who dared enter the playground with glasses on their face. I managed to get through high school with minimal spectacle wearing and minimal teasing, but at some point in my early twenties it became apparent that seeing was a worthy cause.

By then, eyewear fashion had remarkably improved from the round, pink-speckled frames I carried around in my bag for years. So, I started to wear a funkier pair of glasses full time and for a while they worked, helping me see my way through life. But every six months or so, I would head back to the optometrist after work for another check-up, because I could no longer read street signs or the prices of take away items on boards behind the front counter. I would fail the eye test, guessing too many o's instead of a's and they would send me off with a stronger pair of glasses and less money for takeout.

After years of deteriorating eyesight and loads of pairs of new glasses, I was referred to a new optometrist. He identified that my tired and overworked eyes didn't need a stronger set of lenses but a second pair of glasses to help with all the closeup work I was doing during the day. I couldn't read the street signs on the way home because my eye muscles were exhausted, not because they had deteriorated and were in need of a stronger lens. I now have three pairs of glasses I wear at different times during the day for different activities. When I look through the right lens, it makes everything clear. And now I can go years without having to get a stronger script.

I was marvelling over this one day and realised a similarity with my faith. There was a season in my life where I felt like every few months or so I would fall apart in exhaustion and frustration. I would then turn to God and He would graciously comfort me, speak truth to me lovingly and strengthen me generously. Then I would head out quite independently of Him for another few months living my life through a faulty Christian lens. I only had part of the proper prescription. This pattern kept occurring until I was given the gift of the right lens. A lens that allowed me to see the truth of who God is, connected with who I am. I realised I was exhausted from living as a Christian without experiencing His daily presence in my life.

In John 15:5, Jesus says, "I am the vine; you are the branches. Whoever abides in me and I in him, he it is that bears much fruit, for apart from me you can do nothing." Trying to do life on my own everyday apart from God was tiring and frustrating. I'd start out well but my finiteness meant that I'd eventually tire. My resolve would start out clear and purposeful but would become blurry and obstructed along the way. But I wasn't meant to live this way. Jesus invites me to abide in him. To abide means to live or stay somewhere. So, I started to remain in Him and He joined Himself to me, where I was daily supported and nourished.

When I started to see through this lens, I experienced His presence and love more clearly and I started talking with God about the details of my life like I never did before. I experienced deeper and more satisfying relationship with Him on a daily basis. I started to live in Him and He in me like a branch that has been grafted into a vine. A healthy branch bears much fruit and my life started to produce more joy, extra peace and additional strength as a result.

I still need regular check-ups at the optometrist to see where my eyes are at and whether I need a lens adjustment. It's the same with my faith. Good Christian community can provide a routine check-up. Honest and deep relationships can help me see where I might need an adjustment in the way I'm seeing and applying the truth and grace of God in the details of my life. But rather than waiting for these check-ups and doing life on my own in the meantime, I now see that God is with me every day because I get to live in Him. I know what it's like to live in a blurry world and then see things clearly. This is my reality every morning when I wake up before I put on my glasses. Being reoriented to God and walking with Him daily through the trials and triumphs of life is kind of like looking through the right set of lenses. Clearer, purer and more vibrant life is the result!

You make known to me the path of life; in your presence there is fullness of joy; at your right hand are pleasures forevermore. Psalm 16:11

PRAYER

Thank you Jesus that You invite me to abide in You and You in me. Apart from you I can do nothing. Just as a branch on a vine can't be supported and nourished without remaining attached to the vine, so it is with me. I need you Jesus and when I remain in You, I can see more clearly. I get to experience your presence and it brings deep and satisfying joy. Help my faith to not get obstructed by thinking I can do life on my own again. Amen.

Fell Off in My Hand

When I was a child, I loved jumping on the trampoline. We had a small backyard, so our rectangular trampoline was pushed into the back corner between the shed, the garden bed and a brick barbecue. I would spend hours each day jumping and to make it more exciting, I would come up with games to play as I jumped. At the time, I used to watch a TV show called 'It's a Knockout.' This was an Australian game show that aired in the late eighties in which teams would compete in various timed athletic tasks. I would make up my own trampoline version of 'It's a Knockout' and time myself jumping from the brick barbecue onto the trampoline, around the four sides of the trampoline, and then back onto the barbecue.

One day, I thought it would be fun to make this event a little bit more challenging. I decided that while jumping past the garden bed, I'd see whether I could yank out one of my dad's agapanthus flowers. If I made it back to the barbecue with a flower in my hand,

I'd give myself double the points. It was a great idea at the time, but later that afternoon when my dad went to water his garden and found his prized flowers ripped up and lying on the barbecue, I had the realisation that maybe it wasn't such a great idea after all. When my dad approached me about it, I untruthfully replied that they had just simply fallen off in my hands. I started to use this excuse whenever I was challenged about whether I had broken something. I'd just shrug my shoulders incredulously and say, "It just fell off in my hand." This became a family joke and I used the excuse to my advantage for many years.

In recent years, I've been reminded of this story as I consider my reluctance to admit the wrong things that I've done and my slowness to repent and turn to God for His mercy. I talked with a mentor about this and owned up to the fact that I still tend to be quite good at hiding behind self-justification and excuses. She asked me what excuse I use the most often, but I was a bit baffled by her question and couldn't give an answer at the time. Later that day, I asked my husband if I ever make excuses rather than owning my wrongdoings. Nath is very honest and doesn't shy away from the truth, so he promptly answered that I do. When I asked him what excuse I use, he went on to explain that I still kind of say, 'It just fell off in my hand.' Again, I was puzzled by his answer as I hadn't used those words since I was a child. Then it dawned on me, as an adult I don't use that exact phrase, but the same excuse would come out in words like, "It just kind of happened."

I realised that I'd trained myself over many years to excuse and minimalise my sin, and then move on. I'd even proudly described myself as a Christian that didn't dwell on my sin. While I thought this was freedom, it was actually a heavy weight to bear because it brought distance between me and the God I love. It became apparent to me that there's something sweet and precious about confessing my sins to an all-powerful, all-loving, perfectly just and forgiving God, and then receiving His kindness and mercy. This was something that I was constantly missing out on by excusing myself and thinking that I was doing well by 'not dwelling on my sin'.

When I fail to follow God and His ways, I have learned that I need only to return to Him and repent instead of hiding or justifying myself with excuses. In quietly trusting in His amazing grace and mercy, I will find rest for my soul and the joy of my salvation. The words of Psalm 51 have become a sweet prayer for me as I revel in this new way of living. I now confidently approach God with the truth of my brokenness and no longer need to use the excuse, 'It just fell off in my hand'.

Have mercy on me, O God, according to your steadfast love; according to your abundant mercy blot out my transgressions. Psalm 51:1

PRAYER

Thank you Lord for your sweet mercy and your steadfast love that washes me clean from my sin and renews a right spirit within me. Help me to confidently approach you with the truth of my brokenness knowing that in your presence I will find your amazing grace. Amen.

Hearty Hospitality

Warm, old-fashioned hospitality is a treat for your soul. The sort of hospitality that feels like you were lost and finally made your way home, where you are so overwhelmingly lavished with generosity that you can't help but feel connected to the people who have bestowed it. I have been the recipient of this kind of hearty hospitality several times that really stand out in my memory.

One of these times was in a mountainous village up in the hills of Fiji. I travelled there with Nath and a group of his senior high students on a school excursion. When we arrived at the village, the people came out and helped to carry our luggage to their modest homes. They gave us their beds to sleep in and moved into each other's houses and slept on the floor so that we could have the best of what they had to offer. They then provided a feast for us and made sure we had our fill of the food before eating anything themselves. They were so warm, welcoming and affectionate, especially the little children who would hold our hands and sit on our laps. The view from the back door of the house that they gave up for us was the most beautiful scenery I'd ever seen.

When it was time to depart, they put on a farewell performance for us. As they danced and sang, they placed garlands around our necks and smeared white powder on our faces. This was a traditional Fijian way of showing their love and acceptance of us. After a very short time with these people, we felt extremely connected to them as a result of their extravagant and genuine hospitality. I don't remember how long we kept the powder on our faces, but to wash it off felt like saying goodbye to a close friend that we might never get to see again. Our connection was deep and my memories of those people are still strong.

I've experienced a similar connection here in Australia with some old family friends. When I go and visit with them, time seems to slow down and I feel myself physically relax as I breathe deeply of their genuine love and kindness. They have loved my family for four generations and while they're not blood relatives, the last two generations affectionately call them Uncle Trevor and Aunty Evol. They are wonderful hosts who genuinely enjoy providing hearty meals, endless tea and coffee, and good conversation. When you leave their house, it is always with some kind of gift in your hand and an open-ended invitation to return.

As I think about this kind of genuine, hearty hospitality, I am reminded that God is even more generous than these examples. The Bible is filled with descriptions of God's steadfast love and kindness towards His people. It speaks of His lavish, overflowing, bountiful nature. We catch a glimpse of this when we look at the over-the-top creativity and generosity in creation. The heavens truly do declare the glory of God. Of course, the greatest and most generous gift our God has given us is the gift of His Son, Jesus. I love how Psalm 36 describes the generosity of God. In verses 7-8, it says, "How precious is your steadfast love, O God! The children of mankind take refuge in the shadow of your wings. They feast on the abundance of your house, and you give them drink from the river of your delights."

The villagers in Fiji and Uncle Trevor and Aunty Evol are wonderful reminders of God's generous nature and His lavish love and kindness. He will welcome you with open arms, fill you with good things and invite you to return again and again. The connection you will feel to God in all His generosity and genuine love will be deeper, wider, and higher than any other. It might look a little bit like white powder smeared across your grinning face and feel a little bit like the warmth of old friends that you've claimed as family.

See what kind of love the Father has given to us, that we should be called children of God; and so we are.
1 John 3:1a

PRAYER

Thank you, God, for your genuine love and your extravagant generosity towards us. You lavish us with over-the-top creativity in nature and you gave us the greatest gift of all in your son, Jesus. You welcome us as your children and offer us a deep connection with you that is far greater than that of any other. Help me to keep returning to you over and over again to receive the full breadth of your steadfast love and kindness. Amen.

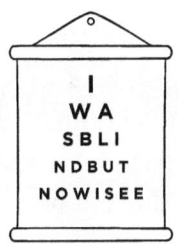

Blinding Experiences

Often the most memorable holidays are those where things don't go according to plan. This was definitely the case for my family one year as we camped on the Sunshine Coast. We arrived, set up our caravan and settled into the daily rhythms of beach life. From the time we arrived, I started pestering my dad to take me fishing. My dad liked fishing but he'd had enough fishing experiences with kids to make him slow to respond. Fishing with kids meant rigging up their fishing lines, helping them cast, baiting hooks and untangling lines. There wasn't really much time for him to enjoy any fishing of his own, and when he finally did manage to cast a line, he knew he would be bombarded with complaints of boredom.

On the second afternoon of our week-long holiday, my dad finally relented, so my sister and I headed out with him to catch some fish. After he had spent a considerable amount of time helping us with our lines, he was finally ready to cast out his own. As he cast his line, somehow the sinker flew off and remarkably came back and hit him square in the eye. Dad dropped to his knees as if he was searching for something in the sand. We asked him what he was looking for and he casually replied that he was searching for his eye. My sister and I did not inherit his calm nature in a crisis and we both started to panic. We confirmed that although his sight had gone completely black in one eye, it was still firmly in its socket. We offered to go and get Mum, but he wouldn't let us leave without first packing up the fishing gear so we quickly packed up, returned to the caravan and told Mum about the fishing accident.

I can't remember exactly what happened next, but I have vivid memories of spending the rest of that week visiting my dad at the hospital where he had to remain with bandaged eyes. I had expected him to be angry with me for begging him to go fishing and to be unhappy about being stuck in a dark hospital room instead of at the beach on holidays. But he wasn't angry or sad! He was happy to see us and optimistic about his circumstances. He made the most of a bad situation and was even cheeky with us and the nurses as we fed him his meals in the dark. He did eventually regain his sight in that eye, and I don't think I ever asked him to take me fishing again! His optimism in trouble was such a great example to me and one that helped me when I ended up in a dark hospital room myself about a year later.

In June 1992, I developed an eye condition called Iritis. I woke up one morning and my eye was completely bloodshot. This was a secondary condition caused by the Reiter's Syndrome which I'd been diagnosed with a month earlier. The treatment was to return to the hospital and spend a week in a dark room having eye drops put in my eye every half hour. My parents came to visit me in the hospital every day just as we'd visited my dad on our Sunshine

Coast holiday the year before. They kept me optimistic about my situation, entertained me with stories from home and allowed me to watch the midday movie on TV.

Optimism and entertainment are certainly helpful in dark times, but even more helpful is knowing the great truths about God. One of these is that He is the light of the world. Psalm 18:28 says, "You Lord, keep my lamp burning; my God turns my darkness into light." When I became a Christian at 14 years of age and then re-committed my life to the Lord at 17, I confessed the knowledge that God was real and that Jesus died on the cross for my sins. I had seen the light in terms of knowledge and was rescued from my sin by God's saving grace, but it wasn't until much later in my faith journey that I really experienced going from blindness to sight in my relationship with Jesus.

When I was in my late twenties and early thirties, I had four difficult births. One of these births resulted in me staying in the Intensive Care Unit (ICU). Although the hospital room wasn't physically dark like the ones treating our eye injuries, it was another blinding experience for me. Somewhere in the chaos of safely delivering my baby girl in theatre and then being wheeled to the ICU, my glasses had been removed and lost in transit. Everything was blurry and I kept slipping in and out of consciousness.

It was through this experience that I started to really 'see' Jesus. I saw Him with me in the operating room; ensuring my baby girl was delivered safe and healthy. I saw Him go with me into the ICU and saw Him in the peace I felt despite the birth not going according to my plan. I saw Him in the doctors and nurses who came in and out of my room as I was forced to rely on their help and expertise, and in my family keeping vigil at the hospital late into the night. I learned that He is kind and loving and able to do more than I could ask or even imagine as I was moved from the ICU the next morning and reunited with my baby in the maternity ward.

Faith isn't just gathering information about who God is, but about seeing and experiencing Him personally through the details of life. When Jesus healed the blind man in John 9, he didn't just receive physical sight. The blind man suddenly saw Jesus for who He really was, proclaimed Him as a prophet and became His disciple. He said, "One thing I do know, that though I was blind, now I see" (John 9:25). The same is true for all who believe in Jesus and start to see Him through their experiences. He turns bad circumstances and situations into opportunities to see and know Him more clearly. He turns darkness into light.

For it is you who light my lamp; the Lord my God lightens my darkness. Psalm 18:28

PRAYER

You, Lord, keep my lamp burning and You turn my darkness into light. I'm so thankful for that. You are the light of the world and You do amazing things even in the hard and dark times in our lives. Help me to see You through all the circumstances of my life and please keep showing me more of Yourself. I am so glad that I can live with the assurance that though I was blind, now I see.
Amen

Familiar Paths

When I was a child, my family would regularly holiday at Hervey Bay. We would camp at the Pialba caravan park in our campervan and we'd enjoy the familiarity of the Bay's tides and the path that runs along the esplanade from Pialba to Urangan Pier.

One year when we were holidaying there, a newspaper crew came and asked my sister, me and two of our friends if we could be in a promotional photo for the local paper. They asked us to sit on the back of a semi-trailer with a huge cut out of a whale that said, 'Having a whale of a time.' We were all very excited and got caught up in our moment of stardom. At the last minute, they asked my sister if she would stand up next to the whale with her arm stretched high in a pose. I remember them saying that they chose her because she had a bright yellow swimsuit on. This never did make much sense to me when the photo ended up appearing in black and white in the newspaper. She was the star of the photo in her yellow swimmers and I sat with my friends at her feet, squinting from the sun, frowning and feeling super envious. I still have a copy of that newspaper clipping, along with many other photos of me as a child holidaying at Hervey Bay.

As an adult, I tend to be a creature of habit, so when Nath and I were looking for a place to camp with our kids I suggested we camp at Pialba, Hervey Bay. We started going there many years ago and enjoyed both a summer and a winter holiday in Hervey Bay for several years. I love the familiarity of going to the same place in different seasons, both in the time of year and in the circumstances of my life.

Each day that we are there, I get up early and walk. I walk under the beautiful weeping fig trees that line the esplanade pathway and remember God's greatness. I walk past the five-meter whale tail, remember my envious moment as a child and thank God for His mercy and forgiveness. As I walk, the water is ever present, either rising or falling depending on the tide, and I think of God's faithfulness. My goal is to reach the pier at a place called Scarness, where I walk out to the end of the pier and then turn around and walk back to our campsite.

One particular summer holiday I was feeling burdened by relational trouble that was going on in the lives of people around me. On that holiday while I walked, I listened to a song called 'Surrounded' as a way of quieting some of my anxious thoughts. The lyrics were simple and repetitive and one of the main lines in the song said, "It may look like I'm surrounded, but I'm surrounded by You." One day as I walked out on the pier, it was high tide and the water went all the way to the rocks, leaving no beach at all. As I stood at the end of the pier that morning, completely surrounded by water, I thanked God that even when I'm surrounded by relational trouble, I'm still surrounded by Him in all His greatness, mercy and faithfulness. He quiets my anxious soul.

That walk each day during our holidays in Hervey Bay is so valuable to my faith. It reminds me of the Songs of Ascent in the Bible. These are a collection of Psalms (Psalms 120-134) which were sung by worshipers as they made the journey up to Jerusalem for the annual feasts. Eugene Peterson in his book, 'A Long Obedience in the Same Direction,' speaks of the faithful Hebrews that made the journey three times each year (Exodus 23:14-17; 34:22-24). He says, "The Hebrews regularly climbed the road to Jerusalem to worship. They refreshed their memories of God's saving ways at the Feast of Passover in the spring; they renewed their commitment as God's covenant people at the Feast of Pentecost in early summer; they responded as a blessed community to the best that God had for them at the Feast of Tabernacles in the autumn" (Peterson, 1980). They sang the fifteen psalms as a way to both express the amazing grace of God and to quiet any anxious fears.

Life is a faith journey. While Hervey Bay is certainly not mountainous and there isn't much ascending to be done on the path that I walk, it defines two times in my year (one in winter and the other in summer) when I vary my daily discipleship and take a time of rest. I remember who God is and where He is leading me. This last winter holiday, I listened to the precious words of the fifteen Psalms of Ascent as I walked the seven-kilometre path from Pialba to Urangan Pier. The familiar path walked over a lifetime of holidays and the daily rhythms of the tide are glorious reminders of who I belong to and that I'm surrounded by Him. The Psalms of Ascent are beautiful truths that provide courage, support and inner direction.

Psalm 125:2 says, "As the mountains surround Jerusalem, so the Lord surrounds his people, from this time forth and forevermore." Just as the mountains served as an illustration of God surrounding the Hebrews, I see God surrounding me on the end of the pier. Psalm 131:2 speaks of a calm and quieted soul and says, "Like a weaned child with its mother; like a weaned child is my soul within me." While I can experience that kind of soul anytime, I experience this calm and contented spirit in an extended way when I'm walking the familiar paths of Hervey Bay.

As the mountains surround Jerusalem, so the Lord surrounds his people, from this time forth and forevermore. Psalm 125:2

PRAYER

Lord help me to vary my daily rhythms at times to remember You in all Your greatness, mercy and faithfulness. Thank you for the Psalms of Ascent that provide encouragement and guidance on my journey of faith. Help me to lift my eyes to You and remember that You surround me in Your love. Please calm and quiet my soul and strengthen me for the journey ahead. Amen.

Sweet Surprises

One of my favourite authors is Bob Goff. He is an American lawyer, speaker, and author of the New York Times best-selling books 'Love Does' and 'Everybody Always,' and my favourites 'Undistracted' and 'Dream Big'. He is an inspiring storyteller who lives boldly and encourages others to live an extraordinary life. I was drawn to his books because of his desire to live whimsically and the fact that 'chief balloon inflator' is part of his identity statement. I think I was also drawn to Bob's books because his stories about his persistent and purposeful nature remind me of my husband, Nath.

Nath persistently pursued me for three and a half years before I agreed to marry him and has continued to faithfully pursue me ever since. One of the ways he's done this is by organising a weekly date night and having a dedicated time to celebrate our wedding anniversary each year. When our 11th wedding anniversary came around, we had four children under seven and our fourth baby was only two months old. We usually tried to go out for dinner and get away for a child-free night, but on this particular anniversary, we were exhausted parents who just wanted to stay home. Nath organised for the three older children to stay with their grandparents for the night and told me that he'd cook dinner for us.

Unbeknownst to me, Nath wasn't satisfied that this was a special enough way to celebrate 11 years of marriage. He approached a friend of ours who worked in hospitality and asked whether he could pay her to cook us dinner at home and be our waitress for the evening. She readily accepted and told another friend of ours about the plan, who then offered to host our anniversary dinner at her house. That way all the food preparation and clean up could happen downstairs and we could enjoy our dinner upstairs on her private balcony.

Nath was stoked with how his surprise was coming together and delighted in blindfolding me on the night of our anniversary to take the short drive to our friend's house. He walked me up the stairs, laid our sleeping baby on our friend's bed, and led me out onto the balcony, set with a dining table and fairy lights, overlooking their garden. Our waitress arrived and offered us first-class service as she poured drinks and delivered an entrée, main, and dessert throughout the evening. It was such a fun and encouraging night, not just for us but also for our friends who helped us celebrate.

Nath continues to delight in finding ways not only to encourage me but also to push me out of my comfort zone and live more audaciously. On my 39th birthday, he gave me a notebook and a cute little pencil case with pencils, pens and other stationery items inside saying it was to encourage me in my writing. Later that day, I received a text message from him telling me to check my email for the other half of my birthday present. I eagerly jumped online and found an email that he'd forwarded to me from Bob Goff. The subject line read, "Short chat with my Wife?" Wondering what this could mean, I scrolled down and found an email from Nath to Bob asking him, as a way to spur on my writing, whether I could have a 30-minute phone call with him on my birthday. In true Bob Goff fashion, he was delighted with Nath's request and simply asked for me to keep an eye on the time zones and give him a call.

I was overwhelmed, to say the least. I was in awe that Nath would make such a request to surprise me on my birthday, but also mortified that I'd have to make such a bold phone call. I didn't want Nath to come home and find that I'd been too scared to call, so I picked up my phone before I could reason myself out of it. Bob answered after a couple of rings and I awkwardly started to explain who I was and why I was calling. We chatted easily about Australia and what the weather was like here at the time and then he went on to give me four points to help me in my writing. He encouraged me to write every day and practice those four points over and over again. He told me that he was so glad I'd be releasing my words into the world and wished me all the best on my writing adventure!

I was floating on cloud nine after the phone call. I was so uplifted by Bob's encouragement and elated that Nath was spurring me on in my dream to write a book. Being surrounded by encouraging and adventurous people who provide experiences like this for me has helped me to live a more impactful and bold life. The Bible has a lot to say about encouragement, spurring others on, and building up other believers. Hebrews 10:24 says, "And let us consider how to stir up one another to love and good works." Christianity is not a faith that God intended to be lived out alone. Encouraging others and being encouraged by others are both central to the life of a believer. Hebrews 10:24 is an encouragement to call other Christians to acts of love and good deeds.

One of the characters in the Bible who is an inspiring encourager is a man called Barnabas. His Hebrew name was Joseph but he was known by the early church as Barnabas, which means 'son of encouragement.' Barnabas excelled in encouraging others and was pictured throughout scripture as being generous, forgiving, kind, and an instrument of encouragement to many. His character is summed up in Acts 11, "He was glad, and he exhorted them all to remain faithful to the Lord with steadfast purpose, for he was a good man, full of the Holy Spirit and of faith" (Acts 11:23-24). Both Bob Goff and Nath are fine examples of Barnabas men. They are glad men who exhort others to remain faithful to the Lord, and they have been instruments of encouragement to me and many others. Our God is the great encourager and He provides good Christian community so that we can go about living the purposeful life that we were made to live. If we take the time to be like Barnabas, sons and daughters of encouragement, we too can bring great help and courage to those around us.

And let us consider how to stir up one another to love and good works. Hebrews 10:24

PRAYER

Thank you, Father, for persistent, purposeful, and encouraging people. Help me to live boldly to do the things that you have set before me. Show me how to stir up others to love and good works for you. Amen.

Abey and Fluffy

When Nath and I had been married for one year, we brought home our first puppy. We think he was a Jack Russell Cross breed, but have no idea what he was crossed with. He was found by some relatives of ours in a box on the side of the highway with a female dog and two other puppies of different breeds. They were looking for homes for the puppies, so we took the one that looked like a Jack Russell and named him Abraham; Abey for short.

We didn't have a lot of space in our lives for a puppy at that time. We were in the process of building our first home, so we were temporarily living in my sister's granny flat, and were both working full-time. To make up for the limited space and time that we had, we took Abey with us wherever we could. He became a very outgoing little puppy and enjoyed meeting new people and animal friends wherever we went.

We eventually moved into our new home where, initially, we had no fences. When we left for work each day we would chain him to a dog run. Most days he would get off the chain though and just spend his days with the various builders that were working in our neighbourhood. We'd get home to Abey sitting at our front door waiting for us. Oh, the adventures that dog had! They say a cat has nine lives, but we often joked that Abey certainly had nine lives as he always seemed to escape dangerous situations safely.

He survived a paralysis tick, an encounter with a brown snake (he was the hero of this story), a run-in with a prized chicken (he was NOT the hero of this story) and an Easter bunny incident where he ate at least eight large chocolate Easter Bunnies; foil and all! We had Abey for 11 years in total. He was present as we brought our four children home from the hospital for the first time and he lived at both of the homes that we built. At our second house, he was notorious for escaping and going on adventures. Before we'd even realise that he was gone, we'd hear a bang at the front door and open it to find him sitting on the front porch!

One of our daughters, in particular, is an animal lover. She adored Abey but was desperate for a pet of her own. For her 4th birthday we bought her a guinea pig which she named Fluffy. She cared for Fluffy really well and even from the age of four was dedicated to cleaning his cage out regularly and taking care of all his guinea pig needs. Abey loved Fluffy, but we suspected that he would have loved to eat him! He would constantly try to get into Fluffy's cage. It was a common occurrence to find Abey with his head stuck through the bars of the cage and poor Fluffy huddled in a corner in an effort to escape him.

Sadly, Abey passed away suddenly when my animal-loving daughter was in grade two. This was traumatic for her in particular, and we were glad that she had Fluffy to help her through that time. About a year after that, while she was away on school camp, a fox or a wild dog came into our yard and knocked over Fluffy's cage. The next morning there was no sign of Fluffy except a few pieces of his fur. When I broke the news about her beloved pet, she was obviously sad. The next day, as she was processing all of this, she told me something that had helped her to feel happier. She pictured Fluffy, lying down peacefully beside Abey in heaven.

She was only about eight years old but was referring to the Scripture in Isaiah 11:6 that says, "The wolf shall dwell with the lamb, and the leopard shall lie down with the young goat, and the calf and the lion and the fattened calf together; and a little child shall lead them." The prophet Isaiah was describing the peace and safety in Jesus' kingdom. He depicts a series of impossible animal relationships that would not exist peacefully in our current world and says that a mere child will lead these animals around. It is a picture of Jesus' kingdom as one of peace, harmony and happiness, with no violence or harm. I love this truth about Jesus. He is the Prince of Peace and nothing under His rule and reign will be able to disturb or threaten peace, security and tranquility for all eternity!

In the meantime, as we center our lives on Jesus, the Prince of Peace, we experience the perfect peace He promises us here in this current world. Philippians 4:6-7 says, "Do not be anxious about anything, but in everything by prayer and supplication with thanksgiving let your requests be made known to God. And the peace of God, which surpasses all understanding will guard your hearts and your minds in Christ Jesus." When you belong to Jesus, you get access to the peace of God which is available in all circumstances. His peace will guard your heart and mind, even in the midst of trouble and disappointment. And when we pass from this world into Jesus' eternal kingdom, perfect peace will be so sublime that even Fluffy the guinea pig can lay safely beside Abey in perfect harmony.

The wolf shall dwell with the lamb, and the leopard shall lie down with the young goat, and the calf and the lion and the fattened calf together; and a little child shall lead them. Isaiah 11:6

PRAYER

Thank you, God, for sending Jesus, the Prince of Peace, to reconcile us to you so that we can experience peace that surpasses all understanding in this life and an eternal kingdom of perfect peace and harmony in the one to come. Amen.

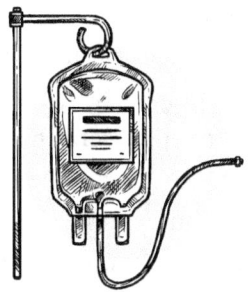

Tonsils Twice

When my youngest daughter was born, I became a mum to four children under six. I was terrified that I wouldn't be able to find the time to feed the baby, let alone do everything else that I needed to do. Somehow, I did find the time to feed her and she was a very happy, contented baby; the perfect addition to our family. Life, however, continued at a hectic pace, and over the next few years, the physical and emotional demands of motherhood only increased.

All four of our children were susceptible to either chronic or recurrent tonsilitis and each became miserably sick with inflamed and infected tonsils. My oldest child had a tonsillectomy at the age of five and the next two children followed suit by having their tonsils removed at the age of four. I noticed the symptoms earlier in my youngest child and because of the family history, the specialist decided it would be best for her to have her tonsils removed when she was only two and a half. The procedure went well and after four tonsillectomies, we had become adept at surviving the recovery process.

During that same year, one of my older daughters had an accident at school while playing a game of tag and broke her elbow. This took us back to the operating room for the fifth time as she needed to have her arm reset under general anaesthetic.

Only a few months later, my youngest daughter started showing symptoms of tonsilitis again. I thought her symptoms were strange given that she no longer had tonsils, but out of habit, I shone a torch into her mouth to check her throat anyway. To my surprise, I saw what looked like two infected tonsils in the back of her mouth. Thinking that I'd gone crazy and that the stress of a hectic few years with sick children had finally caught up with me, I called the specialist surgeon who had removed the tonsils less than a year before. When I explained what I was 'seeing', they assured me that I probably wasn't crazy and that while it is very rare, tonsils can grow back. We made an appointment with the surgeon and he confirmed that her tonsils had indeed re-grown. He decided it would be best to remove them a second time given her recurring tonsillitis.

I was overwhelmed at the thought of a fifth tonsillectomy but my happy, contented baby was also a brave and resilient child. She took it all in her stride and not only underwent a tonsillectomy for the second time that year but also had two more general anaesthetics before her fourth birthday. Between all the infections going on in her throat, she also developed a cyst at the top of her nose. She needed an MRI under anaesthetic to confirm that it was benign and then had the cyst surgically removed. This brought us to a total of eight general anaesthetics between our four children in the space of about nine years!

During these hectic years, my son and youngest daughter shared a bedroom. On their shared cupboard door hung a poster with a picture of an eagle and the verse from Isaiah 40:31. It said, "But they who wait for the Lord shall renew their strength; they shall mount up with wings like eagles; they shall run and not be weary; they shall walk and not faint." On the evening of my son's tonsillectomy, I was waiting for Nath to meet me at the hospital so that we could swap places and I could go home for the night. The following day was my birthday and Nath wanted for me to be able to wake up at home and enjoy a birthday breakfast with the girls before returning to the hospital.

I was feeling physically and emotionally drained and anxious about leaving my son after his operation. As I prayed for him before I left, he seemed to notice that I was feeling sad and something prompted him to quote the verse from his cupboard door to me. He said, "Mummy, they that wait upon the Lord will renew their strength; they will rise up with wings like eagles; they will run and not grow weary; they will walk and not grow faint" (Isaiah 40:31). These words spoken to me by my four-year-old son were like a balm for my weary soul. Through my son, God reminded me that He is my source of strength. I need only to wait upon the Lord and He would renew my failing strength.

I don't know why our family went through so many operations in less than a decade, but as I reflect on those years, I'm thankful for the way they helped me to wait upon the Lord. When my children were small, I rarely had time to stop and I hardly ever sat down. Where did I learn to wait? I learned to wait while sitting in doctor's offices and hospital waiting rooms. How did I learn to wait? By being so exhausted and burdened by the circumstances of my life that I came to the end of myself. I ran out of my own resources and I looked to God for help and waited for Him to work. You might grow weary, but God won't. You may grow faint, but God doesn't. The ever-strong and never-weary One loves to help weak and tired people. The strength that He so generously gives is like rising up as an eagle or running without growing tired.

But they who wait for the Lord shall renew their strength; they shall mount up with wings like eagles; they shall run and not be weary; they shall walk and not faint. Isaiah 40:31

PRAYER

Lord, you are ever-strong and never-weary! Thank you that I can wait for you and you will generously renew my strength. Help me to remember this truth, especially when I'm exhausted and burdened by the circumstances of life. Amen.

Zoe Monster Moments

When my two eldest daughters were little, we would hang out together watching Playschool. It's no secret that I am a Playschool fan. I watched it until I was older than most kids and only stopped because a boy in my class, who happened to live across the road, caught me watching it one afternoon and told everyone at school the next day. When I became a Mum, I was pretty chuffed that Playschool was still going strong and showed daily on ABC Kids.

One day when my daughters and I settled in to watch Playschool, we happened to catch the end of Sesame Street. It was some kind of segment with Elmo and Zoe Monster explaining the word 'mad'. They were talking to each other when Zoe Monster suddenly got mad and had a crazy monster moment where she yelled and carried on. My eldest daughter, who has always been able to express herself well with words, turned to me and said, "Mummy, sometimes you have Zoe Monster mummy moments." Initially I was offended by her statement but she was right. It became a bit of a phrase between us and I would often apologise to her for having a Zoe Monster moment and ask for her forgiveness.

One of the seasons in my motherhood where Zoe Monster made quite an appearance was in the early days of the dreaded "school run." At that time, I had two daughters in grades one and two, my son was in kindergarten and I had a toddler at home. Instead of lounging around waiting for Playschool to start, mornings were now busy and stressful. Getting three children to school and kindy with a toddler in the mix left me grasping at the checklist in my head to make sure everyone had what they needed each day.

During these frantic school mornings, one of my daughters regularly struggled with being easily distracted. It seemed that the more I reminded her of what she was meant to be doing to get ready, the more she found other things to do instead. I would then say things like, "Hurry, we're going to be late." Or, "Hurry, we're not going to make it!" My stress seemed to make her escape even more. When we finally arrived at school, I'd try to get the girls to hurry out of the car saying, "Quick, the bell is about to go!" She'd then respond, teary by this stage, asking me to walk her to class. This meant getting the other two kids out of the car and walking slowly down the long path to her classroom. She'd then cling to my leg and not want to go in.

Her behaviour made no sense to me at all, because I thought that she would be glad to get away from her stressed-out mummy who'd been nagging at her all morning. By the time I'd manage to peel her off of my leg and hand her over to the teacher, I would be feeling guilty that she was late and terrible about the way things had ended. I would then carry my guilt to kindy, drop that child off, and then head home with the toddler and the good intention of stopping to turn to God for forgiveness and help. But I'd get home and see the mess we left behind and the stopping never came.

Over the years, God in His grace has helped me to see that I don't need to wait for the perfect time to turn to Him. He isn't far off and I don't need to have lots of time to be able to go to Him for help. He is always with me. All I need to do is to turn my face to Him in the moment of trouble and let Him reshape my heart and the hearts of my children. God reminded me of this one day when we were making the slow trek down the path to my daughter's classroom.

I stopped halfway there and apologised to God and my daughter about my stress and my Zoe Monster moment. I asked her for forgiveness and we prayed. This took only about half a minute and then she turned to me and said, "Mummy, you don't need to walk me the rest of the way." She hugged me goodbye and happily ran off to class. The next day God reminded me of this while we were still in the car (before getting the younger kids out). Again, I apologised to her, asked for forgiveness and prayed for God's help. Then she said, "Mummy you don't need to walk me down." She hugged me goodbye and happily walked into school with her sister.

I'm learning that the 'win' is not in always getting it right, but rather in turning my face to God in the bad or hard moments for forgiveness and help. As I go about my day with God's help, I'm slowly being reshaped. There is great hope in our messiest monster moments because God is with us and nothing is impossible with God. Luke 1:37 tells of the moment when the angel Gabriel came to Mary to tell her that she had been chosen to be the mother of Jesus, the Son of God. He spoke to her fears and doubts saying, "For nothing will be impossible with God." He doesn't say nothing will be impossible 'for' God (although that would also be true). He says nothing will be impossible 'with' God. He is offering Mary the gift of journeying with God as He carries out His plan of redemption.

As we walk with God, He offers Himself to us too; in the daunting and overwhelming times, in the mundane and monotonous and in our seemingly insurmountable difficulties and pressures. When we're tempted to try and do it all alone, in our own strength, or with our own ridiculously high expectations, we should reach out to Him instead. Stop and turn your face to God and look to Him for help, strength and grace. Reaching out to God in whatever way we can is life-giving and life-changing. Although Zoe Monster still pops up now and again, by God's grace, she is now much more of a minor character in our household with only the odd guest appearance here and there.

For nothing will be impossible with God. Luke 1:37

PRAYER

Thank you, God, that you are with me and that nothing is impossible with You. Thank you that you offer me Yourself and the gift of journeying through life with You. Thank you that when I turn to you for help and strength, you not only help me in those moments, but you change me by reshaping my heart. Help me to reach out to you each day, moment by moment. Amen.

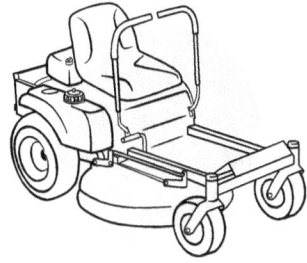

Audacious Requests

Audacity is a word that has come to my attention recently. It means, 'a willingness to take bold risks.' When I think about audacity, I think about my son. He is the only boy amongst three sisters and quite the surprise package. He is small for his age and appears cute and endearing, but he's actually bold, takes risks, and is unpredictable. He is always keen to take on challenges and destroy anything to learn what makes it tick.

One Saturday morning, when he was about six years old, he came to our bedroom door and asked, "Daddy?" The way he said 'Daddy' implied that there was going to be some kind of request to follow and that particular morning was no exception. He asked, "Daddy, can I take the motor out of your mower?" No explanation or persuasive argument was provided; just the question followed by silence as he waited for what he hoped would be a yes. Nath smiled really big and replied, "No, mate." Having received his answer, our little boy said, "Ok," and ran back down the hallway.

This interaction brought the word audacity to mind. It was so audacious for my six-year-old to ask his dad if he could take a motor out of a perfectly functioning ride-on mower and expect that maybe he would say yes. What would make my son bold and daring enough to request such a crazy thing? He knows his dad's character. He knows that Nath is kind and generous and encourages creative thinking. He knows that his ideas are usually met with enthusiasm, and he's had enough positive responses to get bolder and more daring with his requests. He's also watched as Nath has asked God similarly audacious things and celebrated when God has answered those requests with a yes. One of my favourites of these was the piano request.

Nath grew up loving music and had the opportunity to learn the violin at school. He then went on to teach himself to play both the guitar and the drums. Our children, unlike me, have all shown natural musicality and were keen to start learning a musical instrument. When the girls started taking piano lessons through a private tutor at school, we bought a second-hand electric keyboard for them to practice on at home. Unbeknownst to me, Nath secretly longed to have a proper acoustic piano for them to play instead.

One day, Nath told God how much he'd love to own one and asked if God would provide one for us for free. That Saturday morning, I received a message from a friend asking if we wanted a free acoustic piano. She was helping some friends move house who didn't want to take their old piano with them. She had asked God to whom she should offer the piano, and even though she was sure we already owned an electric one, she said that we kept coming to mind. I went and told Nath about the message to see if he was interested and he just smiled really big and said, "Yes, thank you,

God!" He went on to tell me how he'd just asked God for a free piano a few days earlier. When I told my friend she was so pleased that she had asked God who to give it to and that she had listened to His answer.

God wants us to be more like my boy and his dad. We can ask audacious requests of God because we know His character. The Bible speaks of God's character in Exodus 34:6. It says that God is merciful and gracious, slow to anger, and abounding in steadfast love and faithfulness. The Bible tells us that God is kind and generous and we only have to look at creation to see that He is the most creative thinker there is. He is a good and perfect Father and He loves it when we come to Him with audacious requests. Sometimes He might say, "No, mate," because, like my son, we have no idea of the implications of some of our requests. But He encourages us to ask all the same and often, wherever possible, He does say yes for our enjoyment and His glory.

Delight yourself in the Lord, and he will give you the desires of your heart. Psalm 37:4

PRAYER

Lord, help me to delight in You and Your character. Thank you that You are good, kind, and generous and encourage creative thinking and audacious requests. Help me to humbly accept when You lovingly say no and to joyously thank you when You answer with a yes. Amen.

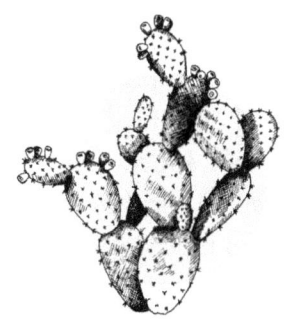

Prickly Pear

Two of my four children experience the world largely through the sense of taste. From the time they could move, they would put everything in their mouths. I couldn't count the number of times that I had to put my fingers into a little mouth and scoop something out that shouldn't have been there. One time I even found a googly eye staring back at me from the mouth of one of my babies. The thing that's special about these two kids is also their zeal for life. They're the type of kids who won't settle for hearing or seeing something; they've got to experience it for themselves. They're deep thinkers and passionate learners but are also a little impulsive.

One time, we set out on what was meant to be a fun family hike at a local nature reserve. We hadn't been there very long when we passed a cactus with some pear-like red fruit hanging on it. As we were walking past, Nath said to the kids, "Did you know that you can eat the red fruits on the prickly pear?" With that, my two 'taste-loving', impulsive children reached out and not only grabbed a red fruit from the cactus but in one swift movement put it to their lips. If they had taken the time to ask Nath a follow-up question before touching the fruit, not only with their hands but also their lips, he would have added that the red cactus pears are covered in tiny, hair-like spines that are difficult to see. He might also have told them that you must wear thick gloves to remove the fruit and cut the tough, spiny exterior off before tasting the flesh inside.

Due to their hasty desire to learn through experience, they both quickly discovered just how many spines are on one piece of fruit. As we started helping them pick out the tiny prickles from their hands and lips, my other two children kept shaking their heads in disbelief, asking why they would do such a thing. The only explanation that the two tasters could give was that they wanted to see what it tasted like for themselves. When we discovered that it was actually going to take quite some time and a pair of tweezers to de-spine their soft little hands and lips, we headed back home, put on a movie, and spent the next couple of hours removing hundreds of spines instead of hiking. Years after this incident, I asked my kids whether they could remember what the prickly pear tasted like? They were both quick to respond enthusiastically that it was still the best tasting fruit they'd ever eaten!

These two kids have a deep yearning for understanding and enjoyment that comes through discovery and experience. The Bible talks about experiencing God like this in Psalm 34:8. It says, "Oh, taste and see that the Lord is good! Blessed is the man who takes refuge in him!" This scripture refers to being active and involved in personally knowing the goodness of God. Trusting in a God whom you have personally discovered is good, even in the midst of difficult circumstances, is taste-tantalizing stuff. God's goodness never fails and never disappoints no matter what circumstances you're faced with. Psalm 34 was written by David while he was a fugitive, running for his life. He experienced God in a very real and incredible way as he drew close to God in a hard situation. The Lord delivered David from the Philistines at Gath and this psalm celebrates the goodness of God, in particular, that God sees, hears, and rescues His people when they trust in Him alone. God's protection and deliverance of David from his enemies was so real to Him that he could taste and see God's goodness.

I've had similar experiences in my spiritual journey where God's goodness was so tangible that I could taste and see it. One of these experiences came when I was suffering from a back injury and was unsure where to turn for relief and help. After struggling along for a couple of weeks, I spent a day at home trying to do what I could with a sore back, which wasn't much. I had prayed to God and asked for healing for my back and wisdom in knowing who to turn to for help, but I was feeling quite downcast as I suffered through the day. There were a number of times that day when I bent over and felt the pain in my back, that I also heard the words, "Call Deanne." I didn't know a person named Deanne so I wasn't sure what it meant, but it was definitely a clear directive and I heard it at least three times across the course of the day.

As I pondered the words that night, I remembered that a friend of mine had a chiropractor friend with a name that started with 'D', so I messaged her to ask what her chiropractor's name was. She replied saying that her name was Deanne. I managed to get one of Deanne's last appointments before she went away on holidays.

Within two days of my adjustment, my body had never felt better. I couldn't help but praise God, just as David did in Psalm 34. I could have said, "Oh, taste and see that the Lord is good," and meant it wholeheartedly! God's goodness is worth tasting. I've tasted it and so can you! It's like biting into a vibrantly coloured piece of fruit that drips sweet, mouth-watering flavour without ever getting any spines in your hands and lips.

Oh, taste and see that the Lord is good! Blessed is the man who takes refuge in him! Psalm 34:8

PRAYER

Thank you, God, that You are so, so, good. Even though difficult circumstances and hard times are part of life here on Earth, Your goodness remains! Help me to turn to You and trust in Your goodness even in the midst of trials. Thank you that we can actively and personally know Your goodness in such a real way that we can taste it! Amen.

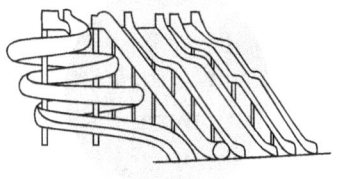

The Wedgie

A few years ago, my extended family met at White Water World on the Gold Coast for a day of fun together. At the time, my own four children were too small for most of the water slides, so they hung out at Wiggle Bay for the day. My parents and some non-swimming uncles and aunties were content to supervise them so that I could go and experience some of the bigger attractions with my older nieces and nephews.

At the start of the day, I felt quietly confident in my ability to keep up with the young teens and be a cool aunty to hang out with. My daredevil nieces, who were about 11 and 12 at the time, suggested that we go on a slide called 'The Wedgie'. I didn't ask any questions, thinking that if they'd been on it before then I'd be able to handle it too. We stood in line chatting about anything and everything as we slowly climbed the tower of stairs to the top. When we arrived, the girls suggested that I go first. Not wanting them to think that they were braver than me I stepped up to what was called the launch chamber.

It was five stories above the ground and unlike any other water slide that I'd been on because you simply stood upright to begin. When the lifeguard asked me to take off my rings and put them in a little bag to be sent down to the bottom ahead of me, I began to contemplate how much power the slide had if my rings could come off while riding. The lifeguard told me to cross my ankles and fold my arms in front of my chest. As I waited for the light to turn green, my niece behind me yelled out, "Aunty Ney, make sure that you don't scream!"

With that, the light went green, the trap door that I was standing on opened, and I started plummeting feet-first down the pipe. I was too shocked to remember the advice of my niece and I did the only thing that came naturally to me at the time - I screamed! The problem with screaming was that as I was barrelling down the slide, the force of the water went straight into my mouth and down my throat. I have no idea how long it took for me to get to the splash pool at the bottom but it felt like an eternity. As I struggled to breathe and was shocked by the intensity of the slide, I was terrified that I was going to drown before I reached the bottom. Just when I thought that I couldn't possibly make it out alive, the braking system kicked in and gave a fast tug on my butt cheeks giving 'rise' to the slide's bold name.

Having a wedgie was the least of my concerns as I emerged from the pipe wide-eyed and coughing, desperate to take in a breath of air. I looked up to see my sisters laughing hysterically and realised how I must have looked as I came out of the pipe. Through their laughter, they came over to help me out and we looked up in time to watch my niece sail gracefully out of the pipe with her mouth closed. My sisters doubled over in laughter again comparing our two very different exits. I probably wasn't in any real danger of drowning in the 10 seconds or so that it took to get from the top to the bottom, but that was the first and final time that I rode The Wedgie. It took me a few hours to recover and longer to see the funny side, but I'll never forget how good it felt to be out of that pipe and taking a satisfying breath of fresh air.

There have been many times in my life where I've been quietly confident in myself, or not so quietly as the truth may be. These have been times when I've clamoured for significance, shouting loudly and insistently about my successes to gain other people's approval. The old proverb rings loud and true that pride comes before a fall. In Proverbs 16:18 it says, "Pride goes before destruction; and a haughty spirit before a fall." When I try to gain approval or significance with my own achievements, it feels good for a while, but it's not long-lasting satisfaction. I know my shortcomings and inadequacies don't match the picture that I'm trying to present of myself and I know that I can't live up to my own expectations because I'm aware of my failings and weaknesses. It's an internal roller coaster when I find my identity in the things that I'm good at and project that image to others when instead the reality is that I'm a weak human being.

The amazing thing about God is that He says in 2 Corinthians 12:9, "My grace is sufficient for you, for my power is made perfect in weakness." I can admit my weaknesses instead of hiding them when I know that my value doesn't come from being good at things or gaining the approval of others. Instead, it comes from God's grace which offers endurance, strength, and satisfaction despite my weaknesses. Christ's power becomes most obvious in the areas where I am weakest.

Jesus gave us a wonderful example of humility when He left Heaven to be born as a baby and then grew up to work as a carpenter and teacher. He went on to ride into Jerusalem on a donkey and endured death on a cross so that we would not remain lost in our sins, but instead, be saved by the love and grace of God. Finding my identity in being made strong by the love and grace of God is so satisfying. It's like coming out of a powerful waterfall, half drowning in my failings and inadequacies, and then taking a deep breath of God's grace and being filled with strength and satisfaction like no other.

But he said to me, "My grace is sufficient for you, for my power is made perfect in weakness." 2 Corinthians 12:9a

PRAYER

Thank you, Father, for Your grace which is more than sufficient for me. Thank you that in my weaknesses You offer endurance, strength, and satisfaction. Help me to live humbly, just as Jesus did, and to know that I can be content with weaknesses, insults, hardships, persecutions, and calamities, because when I am weak, then I am strong. Amen.

Stuck Finger

Nath and I took our children to visit some good friends for dinner. At the time our friends had a baby with whom our kids adored playing. While we chatted with the adults, the kids hung out with the baby in the lounge room and one of my daughters started playing with a baby toy that consisted of little round wooden blocks with holes in them. As she fiddled with the blocks, she put one of them onto her pointer finger like a ring. After a while, she tried to pull it off but found that it was stuck and wouldn't go over her knuckle. We tried pulling it off for her but it was well and truly stuck. We washed her hands with soap and even rubbed some oil on it, but the wooden block wouldn't budge.

By this time, the end of her finger was starting to turn a light shade of purple and began to swell due to the block obstructing her circulation. As we weren't at home and were unsure what else we could use to get it off, Nath took her to the local hospital to see what they suggested. It was a busy night in the emergency department and the wait time was considerable so he decided to return to our friend's house and see if he could cut through the wooden block enough to split it and release her finger.

When they got back, Nath took our daughter out to our friend's shed and they placed her hand in a vice to keep it still. Using a hand saw and his best manual arts training, Nath began to slowly make a cut in the block stuck on her finger. I expected my daughter to be a little nervous about the situation she was facing, but she seemed calm and peaceful and had complete trust in her daddy's sawing ability. Once the wooden block was split in half and her finger released, I asked her if she was scared at all. She confidently replied, "I almost went to cry, but then I thought about how I love to play the piano and I realised that God wouldn't want me to lose my finger." I was baffled by her rationale but also in awe of her simple trust in a good God.

I began to wonder if there had been a bunch of times in my life when I could have simply placed my trust in a good God too, but had instead worried myself sick over something. Later that night as we were leaving, my daughter asked our friend if she could take the broken block home. She said that she wanted to keep it as a souvenir. In Proverbs 3:5-6, the Bible says, "Trust in the Lord with all your heart, and do not lean on your own understanding. In all your ways acknowledge him, and he will make straight your paths." While I know these verses are true, I often trust in myself instead and lean on my limited understanding, so I become worried and anxious about the future. When you trust in the Lord with all your heart, you are acknowledging that God is worthy to be trusted.

King Solomon, often credited with being the wisest man in the Bible, counselled his son to live a life of trust in God (Proverbs 3). Solomon had found that God was so trustworthy that he advised putting complete trust in Him. It is our human nature to trust in something or someone, even if it is our own self, but Solomon teaches us to consciously put our trust in the Lord. This kind of trust is like a child's unwavering confidence in their father's proven wisdom, faithfulness, and love. It's acknowledging that while we can't be sure of the exact outcome in any given situation, we can be assured that God has our best interest at heart.

Nath and I wanted to create a learning experience for our kids that would help cement this truth of trusting in our good God. We decided that for each child's tenth birthday, Nath would take them on a ten-year-old adventure. This meant that one day, anywhere in their tenth year, they would wake up one morning and find that this was the day for their adventure. They'd have no preparation time and wouldn't know where they were going or what they were doing. They would simply have to trust that their dad is a good dad who knows their likes and dislikes, and the things that bring them joy. They wouldn't have any input into the itinerary but would simply put all their trust in their dad and go along for the ride. After this particular daughter returned from her adventure with Nath, I made up a canvas of photos for her room and included the scripture from Proverbs 3:5-6. This simple idea helped form a foundation for her to trust in the Lord with all her heart and not lean on her own understanding.

It was not long after her ten-year-old adventure that she found herself in the predicament with the block on her finger. Her response to trust in a good God who knows her heart came quickly and without hesitation. I love that she kept the broken wooden block as a souvenir because whenever I see it, I am reminded that if God knows that she loves to play the piano and how many fingers she needs to do that, then I can simply trust Him in all things with my whole heart too!

Trust in the Lord with all your heart, and do not lean on your own understanding. In all your ways acknowledge him, and he will make straight your paths. Proverbs 3:5-6

PRAYER

Thank you, Lord, that we can simply trust in You with all of our hearts. Thank you that You are good and we can have childlike, unwavering confidence in Your proven wisdom, faithfulness, and love. Help me to acknowledge You in all my ways because you are worthy to be trusted. Amen.

King Mao

One of my daughters loves sushi and was always curious about The Sushi Train restaurant. One day, when just the two of us were out together, I decided to check out how a sushi train works. We walked in and waited for someone to meet us and explain what we were meant to do. No one came to our aid and I couldn't see any instructions around so I figured it must be easy. I picked up a plate and some tongs and started taking pieces of sushi off of the plates that appealed to me as the conveyor belt went past.

It quickly became evident that this wasn't what you were supposed to do as about four staff members all started yelling out, "plate, plate!" They demonstrated that I was meant to take a whole plate off of the train and not just one piece of whatever I wanted. They then started grabbing the plates that I had taken sushi from and brought them over to me to purchase. I started to laugh at the scene I had created but the staff never even cracked a smile. I explained that I just wanted to purchase four pieces of sushi in total but they insisted that I purchase all four plates that I'd contaminated. We walked out of The Sushi Train with sixteen pieces of sushi and an embarrassing experience.

It can be embarrassing to make mistakes, especially if there are witnesses. The truth is we all make lots of them. Some of my mistakes have meant nothing more than a bit of embarrassment and some extra sushi, but others have been much more costly. No matter how big or small the blunder, my response is usually the same; offer an excuse, play the victim and blame others to justify myself. In the incident at the Sushi Train, my excuse was that I couldn't find instructions or understand the staff. I played the victim and blamed the staff for being unhelpful and rude. I walked out of there in self-protection mode, laughing it off and telling myself and others that it was their mistake, not mine! This is the classic pattern of shame. We know we have made a mistake, and we fear it says something about who we are, but instead of going to God for help, we play the victim and blame others in our effort to protect our own identity (Sondergeld, 2022).

When Nath and I were first married, we attended a church family camp. It was a casual weekend to just gather together and play games, worship God and fellowship with one another. One afternoon, a bunch of our friends started playing a card game. This set the scene for one of my larger and more public mistakes – completely losing my temper. I generally have a calm personality but I'm also quite competitive and I don't like to lose. I love card games and grew up playing a card game called 500 with my extended family. I learned from a young age that the main aim of every round was to claim victory and bragging rights. So, I eagerly sat down at the church camp card table and asked which game they were playing.

The guy passing out the cards said that it was called 'King Mao' and passed me some cards. Then they just kept on playing without explaining any of the rules of the game. I asked how to play but no one said anything as I was passed another card. I soon realised that I received another card every time I asked a question. I then started to receive cards for reasons other than just talking and asking questions, but I couldn't work out what I was doing wrong or how I was supposed to play. With every card I received and every blank stare or mischievous smile I got madder and madder inside.

I was keen to fit in with these people and I was hoping to deepen some friendships throughout the camp, but my frustration caused those goals to fly from my mind along with my patience and self-control. It seemed to me that I was the only person left out of some secret that everyone else knew. I started to feel insecure and inadequate for not being able to figure out the rules of the game like everybody else. So, I lost it! I stood up, threw my cards at the guy who kept passing them to me and I yelled at everyone playing about how immature they all were. I stormed out of the room and ran to my tent to hide.

It turns out that King Mao is an old card game where the aim is to put down all of the cards in your hand without breaking certain unspoken rules. The game forbids its players from explaining the rules to new players so specifics are only discovered through trial and error. A player who breaks a rule is penalised by being given an additional card from the deck. The person giving the penalty must state what the incorrect action was, without explaining the rule that was broken. Sounds fun, huh? Except if you're the only new player in the game who also happens to be the new girl, struggling with feelings of insignificance and insecurity.

I'm now able to see why that card game from over 20 years ago was such a big deal to me and just harmless fun to everyone else. My new husband came to me and suggested that I should apologise to smooth things over, but that made no sense to me at the time because I had already decided it was their fault for playing such an immature game. I had already justified my actions, made my excuses, played the victim and blamed them for my outburst. Even so, I still carried regret over the way that I had behaved that day and I cringed whenever anyone mentioned King Mao.

We all make mistakes because of our human weakness and failures. I've learned that going into self-protection mode by making excuses and blaming others damages the very thing that I long for most - relationship. As God's people, we are not immune from making mistakes, but amid blunders and slip-ups, God promises that He will come close and remain with us. I have a good God who I can go to for help when I make mistakes and I don't need to try and protect myself from the feelings of insignificance and inadequacy that come with them. Hiding in excuses and self-justification is like Adam and Eve covering themselves with fig leaves and hiding in the bushes (Genesis 3:7-8). We all need someone who will look upon us in our trouble, have mercy on us and love us (Sondergeld, 2022). God draws near to me in my mistakes and offers to cover my guilt and shame.

1 John 1:9 says "If we confess our sins, he is faithful and just to forgive us our sins and to cleanse us from all unrighteousness." I've carried shame and regret over my angry outburst while playing King Mao for more than twenty years. I grieved the consequences of my actions and the damage they did to my relationships, but

my grief never brought me to repentance. It hurts to recognise my sinfulness, but when that hurt leads to repentance, it is a pain that frees me from regret and brings me freedom and comfort. As I've asked God to forgive me for my anger and loss of control that day, I have found liberty from my shame and regret. Godly sorrow produces repentance and brings me near to God.

I now know that when I make a mistake, I don't need to blame others in an attempt to protect my own identity, but instead, I can go to God for help. In right relationship with Him, I am strengthened by the security and significance that comes from my salvation. With that kind of confidence, I might even be able to say, "Who's up for a game of King Mao?"

If we confess our sins, he is faithful and just to forgive us
our sins and to cleanse us from all unrighteousness.
1 John 1:9

PRAYER

Lord, I'm not immune from making mistakes. Help me
to own my errors and draw near to You in and through
them. Thank you that you come close, remain with me in
my trouble and have mercy on me. I pray that instead of
trying to protect myself with excuses and blaming others,
I would allow You to uphold me in Your great mercy and
love. Amen.

Undistracted Life

I had the privilege of attending a 'celebration of life' service in honour of my great Auntie Averil. She was my Grandad's youngest sister and she lived just short of her 89th birthday. She was a joyful lady with a wonderful smile and a contagious laugh and she had lived her whole life in the house that her parents built, a house that is now over one hundred years old. I have fond memories of visiting my Great Grandma and Auntie Averil in that house when I was a little girl. I remember sitting with Great Grandma on her day bed with a colourful crocheted blanket, I recall playing the pianola in the dark floral carpeted lounge room and playing with the big doll that Auntie Averil owned. I loved looking at all the ornaments that they kept on the side table with the white lace doilies, and I remember using a patterned glass cup to drink water in the old kitchen.

After Auntie Averil's celebration of life service, I had the opportunity to go back to her house and see it one last time. I hadn't been to the house for many years and looked forward to revisiting my memories there and seeing if anything had changed. Much to my surprise and delight, nothing had changed at all. As I walked up the back steps and into the dining room, I saw the daybed with the coloured crotchet blanket. As I entered the lounge room, the beautiful pianola still stood in the same place on the dark floral carpet. There may have been more ornaments on the side table than I remembered, but the old ones were still there along with the white lace doilies, and the same patterned glasses were still on the shelves in the old kitchen. As I stepped back in time walking through that old house, I had the realisation that Auntie Averil had lived a simple, undistracted life.

At the celebration service, relatives and friends spoke of the love Auntie Averil had for the Lord Jesus and how she had faithfully served Him throughout her life. Seeing her old house after all those years reminded me of a scripture from Colossians 3:1-3. It says, "If then you have been raised with Christ, seek the things that are above, where Christ is, seated at the right hand of God. Set your minds on things that are above, not on things that are on earth. For you have died, and your life is hidden with Christ in God." Auntie Averil didn't leave behind a house full of expensive modern conveniences or a life of luxury. She had lived a simple, undistracted life that was centred on Christ and sought the things that are above.

Not all of us are called to a life of singleness and service in the same way that Auntie Averil was. It is rare for someone to live 88 years in one house and to serve one church, one community and one neighbourhood for their entire life. I'm thankful though for the reminder that the life we live here on earth is not all that there is. It is so easy to get distracted by all the things that this world has to offer that we can forget to seek the things that are above where Christ is, seated at the right hand of God.

The passage in Colossians 3 goes on to talk about putting to death what is earthly in you and putting on the new self. It says to put on compassionate hearts, kindness, humility, meekness, patience, forgiveness, love and thankfulness (Colossians 3:12-17). When we're living our lives hidden with Christ in God, people will have to look beyond the physical things we have around us to see our true riches. They will be hidden in a joyous smile, a compassionate ear, a kind word and a peaceful heart. Colossians 3:4 goes on to say, "When Christ who is your life appears, then you also will appear with him in glory." Auntie Averil was a faithful servant of Christ who lived a simple, undistracted life in thankfulness to God. Now she is being rewarded with an eternity in a heavenly mansion where she will dwell forever with Jesus, her precious friend.

> Set your minds on things that are above, not on things that are on earth. Colossians 3:2

PRAYER

Lord, thank you for faithful saints like Auntie Averil and her simple and undistracted life. Help me to live my life hidden with Christ in God, and set my mind on things that are above, not things that are on earth. As I do this, I pray that I might grow in compassion, kindness, humility, meekness, patience, forgiveness, love and thankfulness. Amen.

Carnival Parade

I have lived my whole life in the city of Toowoomba, nicknamed 'The Garden City'. Toowoomba is known for its traditional Queensland architecture, historic churches, beautiful gardens, and numerous nature trails. The climate is pleasant and those living here get to experience four distinct seasons. Toowoomba hosts various festivals, the most famous of which is the Carnival of Flowers, held each year in September. The Carnival of Flowers runs for seven days and includes a home garden competition, the crowning of the floral queen, steam train tours, and the fun and fanfare of the floral parade.

The floral parade is held on the first Saturday morning of the carnival. People line the main streets of Toowoomba to watch a colourful parade of marching bands, walking groups, and flower floats that represent the diverse community groups in town. As a local Toowoomba girl, I marched in the parade each year from about age seven until I was in my twenties. I usually marched for the Girl Guides except for the few years that I played in the Wilsonton State School Bugle Band. Marching in the parade was a unique experience and one that I loved to be a part of.

It was so much fun to walk the historic streets of my hometown with people lining the sidewalks, waving and smiling at me as I passed them by. The parade would pass several masters of ceremony, usually local radio hosts or prominent people in the community, at different places along the route who would introduce each group to the crowd. Halfway along the route, there would be a grandstand full of invited guests including local and state politicians and important people from the region. The parade judges would choose winners each year from the entrants and floats and these would be announced at the culmination of the parade.

I'm a sucker for simple delights that bring people joy and happiness. What could be more simple and delightful than a floral parade? I love the noisy, fun atmosphere and the array of colour and outlandish sights: oversized mascots, stilt-walkers dressed as butterflies, and thousands of paper flowers on the back of a moving truck. If I'm really honest though, what I love most about this parade is the opportunity for ordinary people like me to feel famous and celebrated for two hours each year. As I'd march by, I'd hear people call out my name when they recognised me, and they'd wave madly at me as if I were someone important. Then for the next few days, people would come up to me and say, "I saw you in the parade!" It felt amazing to be famous for a day!

My daughter's 4th birthday happened to fall on the day of the floral parade one year. We took our places to watch the parade go past and at the end of the parade she turned to me and said, "Thank you, Mummy for putting on a parade for my birthday."

She went on to tell everyone about her 'party' that year, exclaiming how I'd organised a parade for her. She felt very special indeed!

In recent years, I befriended an American girl who was new to Toowoomba. While I was promoting all the great things that Toowoomba has to offer, I told her about the Carnival of Flowers. I particularly mentioned the floral parade and as I was explaining to her how the parade is a unique event that elevates the commonplace people in our community, I was reminded of another parade.

I pictured Jesus' triumphal entry into Jerusalem recorded in the Bible. In the gospel of Matthew, it says, "A very large crowd spread their cloaks on the road, while others cut branches from the trees and spread them on the road. The crowds that went ahead of him and those that followed shouted, "Hosanna to the Son of David!" "Blessed is he who comes in the name of the Lord!" "Hosanna in the highest heaven!" When Jesus entered Jerusalem, the whole city was stirred and asked, "Who is this?" The crowds answered, "This is Jesus, the prophet from Nazareth in Galilee" (Matthew 21:8-10).

I love this picture of Jesus. If I had to pick a time in biblical history to go back and witness, I think this might be it. Jesus was no ordinary man and by this stage in his ministry on earth, he had done some extraordinary things. He was the Messiah or 'Chosen One' that the Jewish people were waiting for, but he wasn't the kind of Messiah they expected. Jesus did some unusual things, like riding into town on a donkey. This parade wasn't the typical celebration of a powerful king, wearing royal robes, and riding on a war horse. It was that of a gentle king in humble clothes, riding on a borrowed donkey. That's what I love about it. The Jewish people weren't expecting their Messiah to be a spiritual leader. They wanted a powerful military and political leader to free them from the Roman occupation. When they realized that Jesus wasn't what they expected or hoped for, they crucified him on a Roman cross less than a week after his triumphal parade.

Jesus' momentous parade into Jerusalem foreshadowed his ultimate sacrifice for humanity: his crucifixion and resurrection. You and I don't need to march in a parade to make us feel important. Jesus showed us that we are important to him by dying on the cross for us while we were still sinners. I can't go back and witness Jesus' triumphal entry into Jerusalem, but one day I will get to see Jesus in all his glory in heaven and shout with all the saints, "Hosanna in the highest heaven!"

For God so loved the world, that he gave his only Son, that whoever believes in him should not perish but have eternal life. John 3:16

PRAYER

Lord, you aren't what people expect and you do unexpected things. You are a gentle and humble king who died on the cross for the sins of the world and who rose again three days later. Sometimes I'm tempted to find significance and importance in things apart from you. Forgive me and help me to remember that your death on the cross for me shows my infinite value to you. Amen.

Special Heirlooms

When I was growing up in the eighties and nineties, we had a cabinet above our yellow, laminex kitchen bench with a glass sliding door. In that cabinet, my mum kept two sets of glass tumblers, one with red strawberries printed on them and the other with green apples. They were our 'special glasses' and we used them for special occasions. They weren't just reserved for one or two important events per year; they were brought out many times and usually marked a celebration of some kind. We used them to celebrate birthdays and when our grandparents or family came to visit. We also used them to celebrate Christmas, a graduation, a new job, a promotion, or any other significant event or achievement. If I came home and saw the kitchen table set with the strawberry and apple glass tumblers, I knew we were celebrating.

The glasses themselves were not particularly special. They weren't made of crystal or fine china and weren't even very unique.

They were probably a common design in a lot of Australian kitchens of that era. It wasn't the type of glass that made them our special glasses; it was the events that they marked in our home. To be fair, the glasses were probably of sentimental value to my mum, but I loved that she was willing to use them to communicate the importance of the people she was celebrating. At some stage, some of the special glasses got broken at one of our celebratory dinners, but that didn't stop my mum from using them because it wasn't so much that the glasses were special, but rather that the people they celebrated were special to her.

As I've become a mum, I've wanted to find ways to communicate something similar to my children. When Nath's grandma passed away a few years ago, we were given some of her china. It was a privilege to gratefully receive some of her teacups and saucers, and since then, I've added some more china cups to my collection. I decided that I would use this 'special china' at my daughter's birthday parties instead of using disposable plates and cups. It's been fun to lay the table with my best white cloth and special china and watch the girls ooh and ahh over the fancy cups and saucers. Each time, I let them know that it's ok if they accidentally drop or break one because, while the china is special to me, it's not as special as the people using it.

Strawberry tumblers and china teacups remind me of how special we are to God. Christmas and Easter, celebrated around the world, mark the birth, death, and resurrection of Jesus Christ. Jesus, God's only Son, came to earth as a baby to save God's people from their sins. Jesus is the radiance of the glory of God and the exact imprint of his nature (Hebrews 1:3). He lived, died, and rose again, and in so doing, made purification for all of our sins. The whole Bible is a display of just how special we are to God.

The book of Romans speaks personally of God's great love. Romans 5:8 says, "But God shows his love for us in that while we were still sinners, Christ died for us." In doing so, we were made heirs with Christ. Romans 8:14-15 says, "For all who are led by the Spirit of God are sons of God. For you did not receive the spirit of slavery to fall back into fear, but you have received the Spirit of adoption as sons, by whom we cry, "Abba! Father!" We are so special to God that He made a way for us to be adopted into His family. We are His royal children, loved, approved, and chosen by the King. He chooses us despite our brokenness, failures, and mess-ups. He loves us, not because we are good, perfect, or loving, but because He is!

A few years ago, one of my daughters decided to get baptised at the age of nine. She loved Jesus and understood the good news of what Jesus did on the cross to rescue her from her sin. When she was talking with one of the church elders about why she wanted to get baptised, she said one of the most profound things I'd ever heard her say. She said, "I used to think that Jesus died on the cross for everyone else, but now I know that He died on the cross for me." Whenever she did the wrong thing, she would get so angry at herself, but she began to realise in those moments that Jesus died to rescue her from her sin and anger and that she could just turn back to Him and say sorry.

This testimony was a beautiful reminder to me that, as a believer in Jesus, I haven't received a spirit of slavery to fall back into fear: fear of not being good enough to be part of God's family. Rather, I have received the spirit of adoption and can cry out to my heavenly Father. When I think of myself as adopted into God's family, I picture coming home to a kitchen table set with the special glasses. This reminds me that I'm special to God, and so are you. If you've been desperately trying to change your behaviour but your efforts are not bringing about the change that you most deeply desire, maybe what you actually need is a positional change. Identity doesn't come from what you do, it comes from who you are related to (Sondergeld, 2022). You need to be adopted back into God's family.

My nine-year-old said it best; Jesus didn't just die on the cross for everyone else. He died on the cross for you, while you were still a broken, messed up sinner. All you need to do is to turn back to Him in repentance. As His dearly beloved child, a celebration with the special glasses and finest china awaits!

For all who are led by the Spirit of God are sons of God. For you did not receive the spirit of slavery to fall back into fear, but you have received the Spirit of adoption as sons, by whom we cry, "Abba! Father! Romans 8:14-15

PRAYER

Thank you, God, that I am special to you, not because of anything I've done, but because I'm your child and you love me. Thank you for demonstrating your great love for me by sending your son Jesus to die for me and rescue me from my sin. Help me to turn back to you, say that I'm sorry, and take up my position in your family; a position which is permanent and will last forever. Amen.

Pet Show

When I was in primary school, I had the opportunity to enter our family's Silky Terrier puppy into a pet show. Our puppy was already very cute but we put a pink bow on her head and popped her into our doll's pram for the pet show. She won 'Cutest Pet' and 'Overall Champion,' and we won a trophy that my sister and I proudly displayed in our room for many years to come.

I am naturally drawn to such fun and frivolous events. A dog show is exciting enough with the various breeds all coming together in one place, but a pet show brings extra chaos as dogs, cats, rodents, and birds all are included, along with the odd pet pig or goat. I'm not normally a lover of chaos, but I'm a huge fan of the random fun and unpredictability created by purposely bringing together these various household pets at a show. So, when I received an invitation in the mail to a local pet show at our community grounds, I immediately entered our two dogs in as many categories as I could. The kids were just as excited as I was, but Nath thought that I was crazy to attempt it and declined to come along with us.

When the day of the pet show finally rolled around, we washed, dried, and brushed our dogs until their coats shone. One dog is a black Jackapoo called 'Toto' and the other is a golden Cocker Spaniel called 'Dorothy', both affectionately named after characters in The Wizard of Oz. Neither of our dogs is well trained, but they're friendly, fun, and very cute. Toto loves people and animals and likes to bark a friendly bark at anyone or anything that he sees. Dorothy is quite timid, but she likes to bounce around on her lead, usually tangling herself with anyone or anything nearby. When we arrived at the pet show, Toto proceeded to say hello to everyone with his constant friendly barking and Dorothy was bouncing around all over the place. It was at this point that I regretted not training them properly and I wished that Nath had come along to help me with the bedlam of our two dogs.

When the pet showing commenced, thankfully there was a separate dog showing arena and another arena for all the other kinds of pets. This helped to settle Toto down as he couldn't see the cats, guinea pigs, birds, pigs, and goats. We carried Dorothy to avoid the bouncing and tangling, and she won first place in the 'Cuddliest' category. My seven-year-old dressed up as Dorothy from the Wizard of Oz and showed Toto in the 'Fancy Dress owner and dog' category. Her cute factor and Toto's resemblance to his namesake certainly helped in securing him first place. We also showed Toto in the 'Waggiest Tail' where he won second place and Dorothy won second place for 'Prettiest Female.' This result was a bit contentious as we think she lost first place to a chihuahua that had yet to win a ribbon. We were thrilled with our prizes though, and I loved seeing my kids revel in the event just like I had at their age with my puppy.

As the event was winding up and the animals from both arenas were getting ready to go home, someone walked their Staffordshire Bull Terrier a little too close to a baby goat. He snapped at the goat's leg, and as the owner pulled him away, it was evident by the goat's bleating and the blood on its leg that it had been injured by the dog. Between the dog barking, the goat bleating, and the owner's anguish, it was quite a chaotic end to an already highly stimulating event.

I wonder if I'm drawn to events like this because they mirror the reality that life can be quite chaotic at times. As a mum of four kids, no matter how much I like order and certainty, life is often disordered and unpredictable. The Lord knows that life isn't always smooth sailing. That's why in John 16:33 He said, "I have said these things to you, that in me you may have peace. In the world you will have tribulation. But take heart; I have overcome the world." It's impossible to have a completely trouble-free life, but you can have a trouble-proof life. You can enter into trouble and chaos knowing that peace is found in Jesus, the overcomer of the world. You can accept each day just as it comes, even the noisy, messy, stressful ones, and have God's help in the midst of it all. The ultimate goal is not to control or fix everything around you; it is to keep communing with Jesus in the middle of the chaos. A successful day is one in which you've stayed in touch with God, even if many things are not in order or under control at the end of the day.

One of my favourite bible verses is found in Isaiah 41:10. "Fear not, for I am with you; be not dismayed, for I am your God; I will strengthen you, I will help you, I will uphold you with my righteous right hand." This scripture speaks about finding strength in God's presence. God is our saviour and protector; He is sovereign amid our calamities and will deliver us from our adversaries. The right hand of God describes a place of strength and authority and is a symbol of God's presence, protection, and blessing. He will use His power and authority to protect and deliver His people and bless them with His presence. I love this promise and I am daily thankful for His presence in the midst of chaos. When life is like a pet show, full of disorder and unpredictability, I'm grateful that His presence strengthens and helps me, and that I can find peace in Him who has overcome the troubles of this world.

Fear not, for I am with you; be not dismayed, for I am your God; I will strengthen you, I will help you, I will uphold you with my righteous right hand. Isaiah 41:10

PRAYER

Thank you, Lord, for your promise to be with me and to hold me up with your righteous right hand. I know that I am not alone in my chaos and that you are always with me, no matter what challenges I face. Help me to find peace, strength, and perseverance in your presence.
Amen.

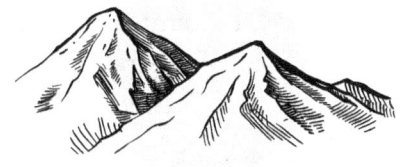

Mighty America

In 2023, I went on a holiday to the United States (US) with Nath and our kids. We spent five weeks on the West Coast and visited the states of California, Washington, and Idaho. As I reflect on our holiday and tell stories of our travels, I've recognised the many times I've used the word 'big' or one of its synonyms to describe various aspects of our time there. The US is about 1.3 times bigger than Australia and has about 13 times the population. There are 50 states in the US compared to only six federated states in Australia. 447 mountain peaks in the US exceed 3000m of topographic elevation. Australia's tallest mountain is Mount Kosciuszko and it stands well under 3000m at only 2,228m. America also has taller trees, higher waterfalls, larger rock faces, and bigger beasts. It astounds me that Americans fear Australia's spiders, yet they have bears, cougars, and moose in their midst.

Driving Route 90 through the northwest of America from Seattle to Idaho was when I first understood just how flat Australia is compared to the lofty peaks of North America. We drove past Mount Si, a mountain that looms over the little town of North Bend, Washington. This mountain, while huge, is not even close in size to one of the 447 largest mountains in the US, but it would easily make the top 30 in a list of Australia's tallest mountains.

Visiting some of California's National Parks really gave new meaning to the word 'big'. We drove our RV up to Sequoia and Kings Canyon National Parks, 13,000 feet (4,000m) above sea level. While there, we were surrounded by groves of the world's largest living things, giant sequoia trees. We stood at the base of the General Sherman tree, the largest tree on Earth by volume, and looked up in awe. General Sherman grows in the Giant Forest, which contains five of the ten largest trees in the world.

We then visited Yosemite National Park and spent most of our time there in the Yosemite Valley, a 1,200m deep trough surrounded by high granite cliffs such as Half Dome and El Capitan. It also features Yosemite Falls, the highest waterfall in North America, which rises 739m above the valley floor. By comparison, Australia's tallest waterfall is only a plunge of about 300m. Looking up at El Capitan and the sheer size of its vertical rock structure was undoubtedly the sight that made me feel the smallest: it is 2,308m tall, 80m higher than Australia's tallest mountain. That day as I stood there and looked up at the spectacular rock formations, I was overwhelmed by the grandeur of God and the tiny insignificance of man.

Nath and I had several goals for our holiday to the US. One of them was to help our kids experience how big God is. There's nothing like going up in an airplane and flying over clouds, oceans, islands, and countries to feel some of the breadth and depth of

God's glory and splendour. Then being able to witness up close the magnificence of some of the world's biggest trees, tallest waterfalls, and largest cliffs helps to give perspective about the brilliance of their creator. The amazing thing about grasping the greatness of God is also appreciating that He, in all His magnitude, wants to have a relationship with us.

At the end of our holiday in America, we visited SeaWorld in San Diego. One of my daughters was fearful of visiting the orca whale enclosure because of the enormity of the animals on the other side of the glass tank. After watching the orca show and seeing the trainers interact with their whale friends, my daughter decided that she wasn't afraid of them anymore. She became fascinated by these huge animals and in awe of the special relationship between the orca whales and their trainers.

Psalm 8:3-4 speaks of God as the most mighty and magnificent being in the Universe. It tells of how God created the heavens with the work of His fingers and set the moon and the stars in their place. Yet, the writer of this Psalm is actually pondering the extraordinary fact that God in all His grandeur is mindful of him personally and cares for him.

The God who made all of the heavens and the earth with His 'fingers' remembers and cares about you too. He is concerned about people to the extent that He seeks after them and is interested in their concerns. He does this even though we are minuscule in comparison to Him. He delights in showing us His glory through the big trees, the high waterfalls, and the large rock faces of mighty America. He lets us see a little of His heart for people in the deep connection that can be found between man and the majestic orca whale.

When I look at your heavens, the work of your fingers, the moon and the stars, which you have set in place, what is man that you are mindful of him, and the son of man that you care for him? Psalm 8:3-4

PRAYER

Lord, you created the heavens with the work of your fingers and set the moon and stars in place. You made the mighty sights of North America in all their grandeur to reflect Your glory and splendour. Yet, you are still mindful of me and care about me and my concerns. Thank you for the deep connection I can have with you despite how mighty and majestic you are and how minuscule I am. Amen.

Aussie Accent

My dad was born in England and immigrated to Australia when he was a child. He left most of his British accent behind in his mother country and instead picked up an Aussie drawl. I used some words throughout my childhood that I just assumed were Australian slang, only to find out years later that my dad had made them up and we were the only family who used them. Other words we used were true Aussie slang, but they certainly weren't words that you'd find in an English dictionary.

We called sandwiches 'zangers', dogs 'panlickers' and an item that you didn't know the name of we called a 'bazooma'. My dad had a nickname for everyone he met, that didn't necessarily have anything to do with their name, it was just the way he remembered them. Often, the nicknames evolved over time and morphed into something completely different. We shortened most words and lengthened others, and rarely used the formal word for anything. Common words in my parent's house were brekkie, arvo, sickie, and snags. We had many sayings and phrases that our family understood but made little sense to anyone else without an explanation. To this day, whenever my family gathers, this language is common amongst us and has been passed on from my dad to his children, and now grandchildren.

In my travels both to the United Kingdom and the United States, I found myself having to explain a lot of the words that I use. Americans, in particular, use a large number of different words for everyday things than we do in Australia. Togs were known as bathers, jumpers were sweaters and the toilets were bathrooms or restrooms. Adding my Aussie slang to these differences made for some very awkward conversations at times.

After travelling for about four weeks in North America listening only to American accents, we visited California to do some sightseeing. One day we went down into the valley of Yosemite National Park and as we were waiting for the shuttle bus, we thought we heard some Aussie accents. When Nath asked the family waiting nearby if they were from Australia, they replied, "Yeah, g'day mate!" Their familiar accent was such a heartwarming sound after so many weeks away from home. We found ourselves gravitating to them throughout the day as if we were friends simply because of our shared accent and home country.

We experienced a similar sense of home when we attended church each Sunday of our holiday in America. We visited three different churches over the five weeks that were all different in size, worship style, and the type of building where they met. One of them was even a bi-lingual church that spoke in both English and Spanish. Despite the differences, in each church, we felt a sublime sense of home. There were familiar things about attending the church services that we could relate to, but more than that, it was the people who seemed familiar. They were God's people, which meant that they were also our people. In 2 Corinthians 6:16, God says, "I will make my dwelling among them and walk among them, and I will be their God, and they shall be my people." The Christians we met in those churches were God's children, our brothers and sisters in Christ. We could relate to them because there was a common language amongst us, passed on from our Heavenly Dad to His adopted children. We had a familial connection because of who we were all connected to.

In John 10:14, Jesus says, "I am the good shepherd. I know my own and my own know me." Sheep listen to the voice of their shepherd and they follow him because they know his voice. My extended family and I can recognise my dad's voice anywhere because we're his family and his language is familiar to us. The same is true for God's children. When you belong to God and are part of His family, you can recognise His voice anywhere too. It's not severed by time zones, physical boundaries, or different languages. Sometimes you might hear it as a still quiet voice in your heart or mind, or as you read God's word in the Bible, or even through one of God's children. No matter how you hear God's voice, you can be certain that it will sound familiar to you, as familiar as an Aussie accent deep down in the Yosemite Valley.

I will make my dwelling among them and walk among them, and I will be their God, and they shall be my people. 2 Corinthians 6:16

PRAYER

The family of God is widespread and includes people of all different nations, languages, and accents. Thank you, God, that you bring us together as your people and that there is a familial connection between us because you are our Father. Help me to listen for your voice and to follow you. Amen.

Kettle Boiling

I grew up to the sound of the kettle boiling. Both of my parents enjoyed drinking numerous cups of coffee throughout the day. I wouldn't be able to count how many times I've watched them spoon coffee into a mug and then pour in the steaming water with a dash of milk. During my childhood, there were many times in a day that my mum would walk over to the kettle, take it to the sink, fill it up, and then switch it on for the water to boil, but never actually make a cup of coffee. There was something therapeutic about the sound of the kettle boiling, even though Mum probably knew that she didn't have time to sit down and enjoy a coffee. As a teen, I remember going to the microwave to heat some leftovers only to find Mum's half-finished coffee mug sitting in there. She wouldn't have time to stop and finish her coffee so she would regularly reheat it and then forget about it.

When I became an adult, I loved the sound of the kettle boiling and I revelled in the smell of coffee, though I never enjoyed the taste. I often felt disappointed about my dislike of coffee as I longed to repeat the simple coffee-making ritual that I'd watched my parents do thousands of times as a child. I wanted to enjoy the act of sitting down to drink coffee, but whenever I tasted it, I couldn't understand how anyone actually liked the stuff.

When I was in my mid-twenties, I travelled to a work conference in Melbourne. Having underestimated Melbourne's unpredictable weather extremes, I was very cold and longed for a hot drink that would help to warm me up. The only hot drink available at the conference was jugs of steaming coffee, so I filled a cup and added milk and a couple of sugars to hide the bitter taste. The hot liquid was so effective at warming me up that I started to develop a taste for it. At the end of that day, I walked to the nearby Starbucks, ordered my very first cappuccino and I've never looked back. Coffee became a comfort that I have enjoyed most days since then, and the kettle boiling is now a normal sound in my own home multiple times a day.

I recently spent time at a friend's house with my family and our host asked if I'd like a cup of coffee. One of my children immediately replied, "Mum never says no to coffee." As I pondered my child's quick response, I started to wonder where exactly I found my comfort. I certainly find comfort in the sound of the kettle boiling, my morning coffee before breakfast, my afternoon coffee on the back patio, and in a cuppa after dinner. I unquestionably find comfort in a takeaway coffee while I'm out, in regular coffee dates with my sister or a friend, and in the offer of a coffee at someone's house. Whilst there's probably nothing too harmful about my love for coffee and the sound of the kettle boiling, it is a poor substitute for the type of comfort that I can find in God.

2 Corinthians 1:3 describes God as the God of all comfort. Verse 4 follows with, "Who comforts us in all our affliction, so that we may be able to comfort those who are in any affliction, with the comfort with which we ourselves are comforted by God." God is a comforting God. His comfort is not just a fleeting feeling, like a hot coffee on a cold day, but a lasting source of peace and strength. It is a deep and abiding presence that brings hope in all circumstances.

This type of comfort is not just for us; we can provide comfort to others because we have received comfort from God. The Greek word for "comfort" means "to come alongside." This is what God does for me and what He calls me to do for others. He comforts me as I read His word and pray each day, usually with my coffee. As I've come alongside others and offered them comfort in hard times, it's often been at a coffee shop or in someone's home with a mug in my hand. Coffee is a fleeting comfort at best, but God is our ultimate source of comfort. Through His word, the Bible, we have access to countless promises that offer lasting words of comfort. I want these promises to become as normal and comforting to me as the sound of the kettle boiling, and to actively share them with others as easily as saying yes to a coffee.

Blessed be the God and Father of our Lord Jesus Christ,
the Father of mercies and God of all comfort.
2 Corinthians 1:3

PRAYER

Thank you, God, for earthly comforts like coffee. Help me to recognise that earthly comforts are momentary compared to the comfort You give. Thank you for the deep and abiding source of peace, strength, and hope that You bring. Help me to receive it readily and to share it easily with others. Amen.

Magical Worlds

I love predictable movies with happy endings and long for magical lands that offer happiness like a prize. According to its slogan, Disneyland is the happiest place on earth, and even though I live in Australia, I've experienced its magic three times! My first visit was in California when I visited the West Coast of America on a "G'day USA" school trip in 1998. The second visit was in Paris on a stop-over to London. Most recently, I had the opportunity to go once again to Disneyland in California, this time with Nath and our four kids. I've also occasionally held season passes for Dream World on the Gold Coast, which promises to create happy memories that will last a lifetime. I feel happy just thinking about walking through those gates to the magical world of happiness that waits within!

It came as a surprise to me early in my Christian journey to find that the Bible has a different measure of happiness or joy than I do. In James 1:2-3 it says, "Count it all joy, my brothers, when you meet trials of various kinds, for you know that the testing of your faith produces steadfastness." The reality is that since the fall of humanity, which happened right back in the Garden of Eden with Adam and Eve, trials have been a part of life even at the happiest places on Earth.

I'm a glass-half-full kind of person but I'm also a realist, and the reality is that there are plenty of trials to face in the magical lands that I love so much. On the first two occasions that I visited Disneyland, I was a student who worked part-time with limited funds. I was delighted to find that the entry fee to this fantasy land was so affordable that even an impoverished student like me could indulge. But something magical happens to the prices after you pass through the gate and it becomes so expensive that you almost need to take out a Disneyland mortgage to be able to eat and drink for the day. The hour-and-a-half waiting times can be another unexpected trial at this happy place. It's ok if, like me, you love a chat and can pass the time by incessantly talking to those around you, but for some reason children and easily exasperated parents don't miraculously become more patient and self-controlled in the long line-up for a magical attraction.

Then there is the kind of trial I faced on the musical cruise called Splash Mountain. I first visited Disneyland California in the middle of January where winter temperatures average about 13 degrees Celsius. While this isn't exceptionally cold, it's also not pleasant weather to walk around wet all day. Splash Mountain is a log-flume ride that ends in a five-story drop. I noticed at the entry to the ride that they were selling ponchos, but as I was a student and needed to save every penny, I decided to pass on the poncho and just work out which seat would allow me to get the least wet.

I determined that the riders at the back seemed only to get a little splash or spray, while those who opted for the front could expect to get soaked.

When it was my time to ride, I jumped in the back of a log behind a rider who was considerably bigger than me. We cruised around a whimsical world filled with classic characters and songs and then I prepared my smile for the big finale: the photo shoot as we tumbled out of the dark and down a five-story drop to the bottom! My photo on that ride was the best of the day! I smiled big and was in clear view of the camera as the person in front of me completely bent over. This also meant that the splash went straight over their back and completely soaked me! It was right at that moment that I decided passing on the poncho was not my wisest decision. I had to spend the next hour or so trying to dry myself under a hand dryer in the bathroom which used up my precious Disneyland time.

At the end of the day when our group gathered back at the bus, I found that my annoyingly organised and efficient older sister had planned out her day and so had seen far more of the park than me, had brought a raincoat in her backpack to use on Splash Mountain, and had collected a bunch of free or cheap souvenirs like postcards and park maps to scrapbook her happy memories. I still felt damp and hungry and had spent my days allowance on Mickey Mouse ears that I'd never wear again outside of Disneyland.

Although the trials of Disneyland are very superficial, the truth remains that life on earth is filled with trials and tests that we can't escape. We have all experienced trials and testing in many and varied ways, yet I and many others still long for a truly happy place. C.S. Lewis famously said, "If we find ourselves with a desire that nothing in this world can satisfy, the most probable explanation is that we were made for another world" (Lewis, 2012). The last book of the Bible, Revelation, is a book of prophecy that speaks (amongst other things) about Heaven. It speaks of richness, provision, and peace, and tells of gladness, life, health, and restoration. Revelation describes a place that is centred on God, where God's people get to see Him clearly, and forever be with Him.

Disneyland might be the happiest place on earth, but Mickey Mouse is no substitute for God. I look forward with great anticipation to the day when all my desires for happiness will be truly satisfied in the richness of life in Heaven with God. In the last two lines of the book 'The Last Battle', the final book in the Chronicles of Narnia series by C.S. Lewis, it says, "But for them it was only the beginning of the real story. All their life in this world and all their adventures in Narnia had only been the cover and the title page: now at last they were beginning Chapter One of the Great Story which no one on earth has read: which goes on forever: in which every chapter is better than the one before" (Lewis, 1995). While I wait for my story here on earth to end and the great story of heaven to begin, I will hold onto the hope that lies within the last line of the greatest book ever written: The Bible. "The grace of the Lord Jesus be with all. Amen" (Revelation 22:21).

And night will be no more. They will need no light of lamp or sun, for the Lord God will be their light, and they will reign forever and ever. Revelation 22:5

PRAYER

Lord, thank you for happy stories and places here on this earth, but help me to remember that true and lasting happiness only comes from life with You, both now and in eternity. I pray that with your help and by your grace I can count it all joy when I face trials of various kinds. You are producing in me stamina and endurance to stay the course, and one day, I will receive the greatest prize of all: the crown of everlasting life.
Amen.

References

In order of appearance

Sondergeld, P. (2022). *Becoming You.* Peter Sondergeld Ministries. Page 30

Keller, T. (2000, March 5). *Psalms: The Songs of Jesus* [Audio podcast]. Retrieved from https://podcast.gospelinlife.com/e/praying-our-fears-1572025713/

Peterson, E. H. (1980). *A Long Obedience in the Same Direction.* InterVarsity Press.

Sondergeld, P. (2022). *Becoming You.* Peter Sondergeld Ministries. Page 26

Sondergeld, P. (2022). *Becoming You.* Peter Sondergeld Ministries. Page 29

Sondergeld, P. (2022). *Becoming You.* Peter Sondergeld Ministries. Page 157

Lewis, C. S. (2012). *Mere Christianity.* William Collins. Page. 135-137

Lewis, C. S. (1995). *The Last Battle.* Scholastic ed. New York, Scholastic. Page 184.

Scripture Index

Introduction – Ordinary Stories of Europe
    Revelation 21:6
    Isaiah 40:8

1. A Father's Applause – "God is With Us"
    Joshua 1:9
    Deuteronomy 31:6
    Matthew 1:22-23
    Matthew 28:20b

2. Hide and Seek – "Place of Refuge"
    Genesis 3:8-9
    Psalm 73:28

3. Bugle Bogas – "God of Light"
    John 12:35-36
    1 John 1:6-7

4. Bag Carrier – "Very Present Help"
    Psalm 121:1-2

5. Sickness Benefits – "Good Shepherd"
    Psalm 23:1-4

6. Glow Worm – "Shield of Protection"
    Psalm 3:2-5

7. Night Sky – "God Hems Me In"
   Psalm 139:5

8. Top Dog – "Generous Master"
   Matthew 20:1-16
   Matthew 19:30
   Ephesians 2:8

9. Lady Shave – "All-Knowing"
   Psalm 139:1-3

10. Mail Box – "God of Laughter"
    Proverbs 17:22
    Ecclesiastes 3:4
    Genesis 21:6

11. Hungry Jacks Origins – "God at Work"
    Proverbs 16:9
    Psalm 37:23-24

12. The Proposal – "Extravagantly Loving"
    Zephaniah 3:17

13. New Lenses – "God of Life"
    John 15:5
    Psalm 16:11

14. Fell Off in My Hand – "Sweet Mercy"
    Psalm 51:1

15. Hearty Hospitality – "Lavishly Kind"
    Psalm 36:7-8
    1 John 3:1a

16. Blinding Experiences – "God of Sight"
    John 9:25
    Psalm 18:28

17. Familiar Paths – "Surrounding God"
    Exodus 23:14-17
    Exodus 34:22-24
    Psalm 125:2

18. Sweet Surprises – "God of Encouragement"
    Hebrews 10:24
    Acts 11:23-24

19. Abey and Fluffy – "Prince of Peace"
    Isaiah 11:6
    Philippians 4:6-7

20. Tonsils Twice – "Ever-Strong"
    Isaiah 40:31

21. Zoe Monster Moments – "Ever-Present"
    Luke 1:37

22. Audacious Requests – "Gift Giver"
    Exodus 34:6
    Psalm 37:4

23. Prickly Pear – "Perfectly Good"
    Psalm 34:8

24. The Wedgie – "All-Powerful"
    Proverbs 16:18
    2 Corinthians 12:9a

25. Stuck Finger – "Trustworthy"
    Proverbs 3:5-6

26. King Mao – "Intimately Near"
    1 John 1:9

27. Undistracted Life – "Treasure in Heaven"
    Colossians 3:12-17
    Colossians 3:1-3

28. Carnival Parade – "Humble King"
    Matthew 21:8-10
    John 3:16

29. Special Heirlooms – "God's Chosen Children"
    Hebrews 1:3
    Romans 5:8
    Romans 8:14-15

30. Pet Show – "God in Control"
    John 16:33
    Isaiah 41:10

31. Mighty America – "Majestic Creator"
    Psalm 8:3-4

Scripture Index

32. Aussie Accent – "God Speaks"
    John 10:14
    2 Corinthians 6:16

33. Boiling Kettle – "Comforter"
    2 Corinthians 1:3

34. Magical Worlds – "Everlasting Life"
    James 1:2-3
    Revelation 22:21
    Revelation 22:5

www.ingramcontent.com/pod-product-compliance
Lightning Source LLC
Chambersburg PA
CBHW051439290426
44109CB00016B/1616